The Official British Rail Book of

TRAINS

This book is to be returned
the last date stamp

for Young People
Michael Bowler

The Official British Rail Book of
TRAINS
for Young People
Michael Bowler

Hutchinson

London Melbourne Sydney Auckland Johannesburg

Hutchinson Children's Books Ltd
An imprint of the Hutchinson Publishing Group
17–21 Conway Street, London W1P 6JD

Hutchinson Publishing Group (Australia) Pty Ltd
16–22 Church Street, Hawthorn, Melbourne, Victoria 3122,
Australia

Hutchinson Group (NZ) Ltd
32–34 View Road, PO Box 40–086, Glenfield, Auckland 10

Hutchinson Group (SA) Pty Ltd
PO Box 337, Bergvlei 2012, South Africa

First published 1985
© text Hutchinson Children's Books 1985
© illustrations see acknowledgements

Phototypeset in Linotron Plantin
by Input Typesetting Ltd, London

Printed and bound in Italy by Amilcare Pizzi S.p.A. 1985

British Library Cataloguing in Publication Data

Bowler, Michael
    The official British Rail book of trains.
    1. Locomotives—Great Britain—History
I. Title
625.2′6′0941   TJ603.4.G7
ISBN 0 09 161511 9

Contents

Acknowledgements

The majority of the photographs used in this book are from British Rail's own archives and the author would like to thank his colleagues, especially those on the London Midland and Eastern Regions, for their assistance.

Copyright of the remaining pictures is as follows:

Science Museum Pages 10 (*top and bottom*); 11; 12 (*top left, top right and bottom*); 13 (*top*); 14 (*top*); 14/15 (*bottom*); 15 (*top*); 16/17 (*bottom*); 17 (*top*); 22; 23; 24 (*top, centre and bottom*); 30 (*top left*); 69 (*bottom*).

Beamish Open Air Museum Pages 18/19 (*bottom*).

Illustrated London News Pages 57 (*bottom*); 81 (*top*).

Northern Echo, Darlington Page 93 (*bottom*).

Yorkshire Post Page 109 (*centre*).

Topical Press Pages 110/111.

Fox Photos Page 112 (*top*).

Daily Sketch Page 117 (*top*).

Allied Newspapers, Manchester Page 115 (*top left*).

Norman Childs Photography, Hemel Hempstead Page 148 (*top right*).

LCGB Ken Nunn Collection Pages 46 (*bottom*); 68 (*top right and bottom*); 72 (*centre and bottom*); 73 (*top left and top right*); 96 (*top*); 108 (*centre*).

Colour-Rail Page 95 (*top*).

E. S. Russell/Colour-Rail Page 70 (*centre*).

L. Hanson/Colour-Rail Page 82.

J. G. Dewing/Colour-Rail Page 94 (*bottom*).

K. H. Leech/Colour-Rail Pages 98 (*top*); 106 (*centre*).

D. R. Barber/Colour-Rail Page 99 (*top*).

J. A. Whaley/Colour-Rail Page 106 (*top*).

J. F. Traxler/Colour-Rail Page 107 (*bottom*).

S. C. Townroe/Colour-Rail Page 118/119.

J. M. Jarvis/Colour-Rail Page 126.

T. J. Edgington/Colour-Rail Page 127 (*bottom*).

A. E. R. Cope/Colour-Rail Page 134 (*bottom*).

M. C. Burdge Pages 71 (*top, centre and bottom*); 135 (*top left*); 136 (*top right and bottom*); 137 (*centre*).

H. C. Casserley Pages 65 (*bottom*); 81 (*bottom*).

H. C. Casserley Collection Pages 95 (*bottom*); 108 (*top*).

Keith Jackson Pages 98 (*bottom*); 106 (*bottom*); 107 (*top and centre*); 109 (*top*).

N. D. Mundy Page 74 (*centre*).

W. S. Sellar Page 83.

Author Page 21 (*top*); 55 (*bottom*); 70 (*bottom*); 114 (*bottom*); 135 (*centre left, centre right and bottom*); 136 (*top left*); 137 (*top and bottom*).

Author's Collection Page 51 (*bottom*); 92 (*top left*); 132 (*bottom left*).

Introduction

This book is a 200 years-long journey by train. It begins slowly and is hauled by horses at first; for over a century powerful steam locomotives are in charge; then, during the past 25 years, diesel and electric traction take over.

The appearance of the train changes dramatically, speeds increase from little more than walking pace to the 200 kph of today's high speed trains. But whatever technical alterations take place, the sheer excitement of a train journey remains the same. And the journey continues into the future . . .

Michael Bowler

Diesel replaces steam in the early 1960's. An English Electric Type 4 diesel overtakes a Coronation class 4–6–2.

1 In the very beginning

Britain's railways were born in the North East of England. They were not 'invented' suddenly; nor did they spring, fully formed, into an astonished world. What happened was a gradual evolution of ideas, both in methods of transport and in the use of steam power, which eventually fused together and brought about the railway system we know today.

The Ancient Greeks understood that wheeled vehicles ran more smoothly if they could be guided along. So they cut grooves in the centres of stone blocks and placed them in parallel lines. Traces can still be found all over Greece. Even then the idea wasn't new: it dated back at least as far as Babylonian times.

Georgius Agricola, a German with a Latin name, published a book about mining called *De Re Metallica* in 1516. Within its pages was an illustration of a four-wheeled truck designed to run on rails. In Britain, waggonways using wooden rails were first laid at the beginning of the seventeenth century. Their purpose was to carry coal from pits to the nearest navigable river. Roads were little more than muddy tracks at that time and the only way to transport goods long distances, from Newcastle to London for instance, was by ship along the coast. Getting your goods to the coastal port presented no problem once you got them to a decent-sized river. It was reaching the river that was the problem.

Here is a model of Richard Trevithick's pioneer engine built in 1803. The locomotive which ran at Penydarren the following year was based on the same design.

Waggonways were the answer. They were primitive affairs consisting of wooden tracks laid on land that sloped gently down to the nearest river. Loaded waggons were carried downhill by gravity to the water's edge where the contents were unloaded into barges. Horses then pulled the empty waggons back uphill. The earliest use of this method, and the first recorded 'railway' in Britain, was a line 3.2 km (2 miles) long at Wollaton near Nottingham. It was built by Huntingdon Beaumont sometime between October 1603 and October 1604 to carry coal from pits at Strelley. A few years later Beaumont introduced waggonways to the Newcastle area, although eventually 'he consumed all his money and rode home upon his light horse'.

Over a century later, the Ravensworth Waggonway in County Durham built the world's first railway viaduct when it extended its line across Tanfield Moor. Known as the Causey Arch, it had a span of 31 m (102 ft), was 18 m (60 ft) high, and built to the design of Ralph Wood, the local stone-mason. Ralph built to last; this, the earliest major railway structure, still stands today.

All these pioneer waggonways were laid over private property. Coal mining took place on the sprawling acres of the landed gentry of the day and the Lord of the Manor needed no one's permission to build as he pleased. In 1758 a significant move took place. The

'Captain Dick's Puffer', Trevithick's steam-powered road carriage built about 1802.

(*Left*) The Causey Arch at Tanfield, Co. Durham was built in 1727 to carry a wooden waggonway. It was the world's first railway bridge and is still in existence.

Middleton Railway, a private colliery line near Leeds, became the first railway to be authorized by Act of Parliament. This allowed it to buy land to extend the line beyond its owner's boundaries, but at the same time imposed certain conditions. Adequate fencing to protect the public from accidentally stumbling onto the tracks was one. It's a regulation by which British Rail must still abide today, over 200 years later.

By the year 1800 there were about 2,400 km (1,500 miles) of industrial railway in Britain. This was made up of dozens of short lines dotted around the country and almost all separated from each other. They had altered little in character or scope in the previous two centuries. Within the next 50 years their successors would have changed the face of Britain and revolutionized transport across the world.

Iron was one of the keys to the great leap forward. For by now the Industrial Revolution was under way, and smoking chimneys and roaring blast furnaces sprouted from the peaceful green country-

(*Left*) The Surrey Iron Railway was the first public goods railway in the world to be authorized by Act of Parliament. It opened on 26th July 1803 and, as this poster says, was 'for the use of the public on payment of the following tolls'.

SURREY
Iron Railway.

The COMMITTEE of the SURREY IRON RAILWAY COMPANY,

HEREBY, GIVE NOTICE,. That the BASON at *Wandsworth*, and the Railway therefrom up to *Croydon* and *Carſhalton*, is now open for the Uſe of the Public, on Payment of the following Tolls, *viz.*

For all Coals entering into or going out of their Bason at Wandsworth,	*per Chaldron,*	3d.
For all other Goods entering into or going out of their Bason at Wandsworth	*per Ton,*	3d.

For all GOODS carried on the said RAILWAY, as follows, viz.

For Dung,	*per Ton, per Mile,*	1d.
For Lime, and all Manures, (except Dung,) Lime-ſtone, Chalk, Clay, Breeze, Aſhes, Sand, Bricks, Stone, Flints, and Fuller's Earth,	*per Ton, per Mile,*	2d.
For Coals,	*per Chald. per Mile,*	3d.
And, For all other Goods,	*per Ton, per Mile,*	3d.

By ORDER of the COMMITTEE,
W. B. LUTTLY,
Clerk of the Company.

Wandsworth, June 1, 1804.

BROOKE, PRINTER, No. 35, PATERNOSTER-ROW, LONDON.

Photography had not been invented in 1808 when Trevithick's *Catch me who can* made its exhibition runs. The exact appearance of the engine is therefore uncertain.

(*Above left*) A reconstruction which can be seen in the Science Museum.

(*Above*) One of the original handbills, a similar design was used on Trevithick's visiting cards.

(*Left*) A drawing, made at the time, showing *Catch me who can* trundling around its circular track near Torrington Square in London.

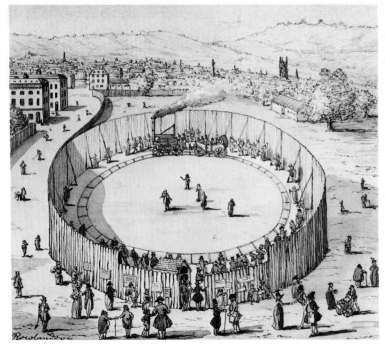

The world's first commercially successful steam locomotives ran on the Middleton Railway, near Leeds, in 1812. They were built to the Blenkinsop/Murray rack system.

(*Above*) A train of coal waggons.

(*Left*) A close-up of the only survivor of this system, a set of wheels now on show at the National Railway Museum, York. The central cogwheels gripped the teeth set in the rack at the side of the rails.

side. In 1767 the pioneer Coalbrookdale Ironworks in Shropshire first strengthened wooden rails by fitting cast iron plates to them. Nine years later cast iron rails were forged at Sheffield. Wooden rails had provided a notoriously unstable surface for guiding waggons, which frequently slipped off. Now with the introduction of iron two methods of keeping them on the rails were devised. One was the plateway where the rails were L-shaped and the wheels of the waggon were plain. Here the wheels fitted within the uprights of the L. The other system is more recognizable. Named after its inventor, William Jessop, the rails were square but the waggon wheels had flanges on their inside edges. The wheel rims ran along the top of the rails and the flanges fitted snugly inside. The principle behind Jessop's rail is still used by the railways of the world today.

So now there were railways that could carry waggons easily and efficiently, but the only power to haul them was still the horse. There used to be a popular story that James Watt was gazing at a boiling kettle one day and all at once realized that if you put wheels on it you had a steam locomotive. He didn't! The steam engine took a little longer than that to evolve.

In 1712 Thomas Newcomen built a stationary beam engine worked by steam power to pump water from a mine at Dudley Castle. It was a colossal affair. From one end of the massive beam hung pump rods. The weight of the rods pulled down that end of the beam. At the other end a piston hung down into an open-topped cylinder. Low-pressure steam was pushed into this cylinder and condensed by being sprayed with cold water. This created a partial vacuum beneath the piston, air pressure acted on top to force it down and, hey presto, the whole beam end came down lifting the pumping rods at the other end. Once pressure equalized, the heavy rods pulled the beam down once more and the whole process began again. It was certainly impressive, but just a bit too big to run on rails.

Enter James Watt. He built a separate condenser, which meant the cylinder could be closed off and kept permanently hot, and steam, rather than air, pressure used to move the piston. Valves were built into the closed cylinder to let steam enter on one side of the piston or the other, allowing it to be pushed in either direction. Watt and his partner Matthew Boulton patented their invention, took the money when anyone used it, and grew rich. Invention for its own sake wasn't for them.

(*Above*) William Hedley's *Puffing Billy* was built in 1813 and ran for 50 years. It is now in the Science Museum.

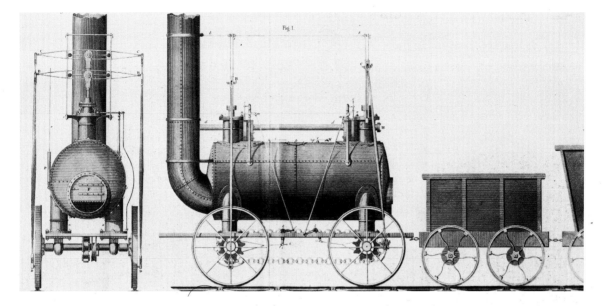

(*Above*) One of George Stephenson's first locomotives.

(*Below*) A busy scene at Hetton Colliery in about 1822. Already the steam locomotive is part of the industrial landscape.

But it was for Cornishman Richard Trevithick, the man who with much justification has been called 'the father of the steam locomotive'. Boulton and Watt's patents expired in 1800 and Trevithick developed their invention to its logical conclusion. If you have a steam-powered piston that can move backwards and forwards and can be coupled to a wheel . . . why, then mount the engine on the wheels and let the whole lot propel itself along.

It wasn't quite as easy as that but Trevithick cracked it. His first attempt was actually a road carriage that looked like a dustbin turned on its side with an assortment of wheels added! 'Captain Dick's Puffer', as it was called, performed well on its first outing, steaming merrily along at an outstanding 12 to 16 kph (8 to 10 mph). 'Captain Dick' was well pleased and, flushed with triumph, adjourned to the local pub to drink his engine's health. Unfortunately he and his friends drank too many other toasts and time slipped away. Outside, like a neglected infant, the new engine's boiler boiled dry and the whole contraption exploded. It was a sad end to a grand day.

Trevithick was undaunted. In 1802 he built a pumping engine which worked at the high pressure of 10.2 kg/cm² (145 lb/in²). This was nearly ten times atmospheric pressure but the cylinder was only 178 mm (7 ins.) in diameter. A year later he applied his work to a railway locomotive. It was built at the famous Coalbrookdale Ironworks and, although no evidence has been found to show that it actually ran there, it was undoubtedly the world's first railway locomotive.

Trevithick's second locomotive, of similar design, was constructed while he was employed at Penydarren Ironworks near Merthyr Tydfil in South Wales. On 22nd February 1804 the Penydarren locomotive hauled 10 tons of iron, 70 men and 5 extra waggons for 15 km at 8 kph (9½ miles at 5 mph).

'It works exceeding well,' wrote Trevithick to a friend, 'and is much more manageable than horses.' Well it did, and it was, but it also crunched up the track. So did Trevithick's third engine ordered by Wylam Colliery in the North-East. They were too heavy for the poor quality track, but had proved that iron wheels would run on iron rails. Trevithick's locomotives also had one other distinctive innovation: a chimney which carried away exhaust steam and improved the draught to the fire. Watt would have patented that idea and made millions. Trevithick probably didn't even think of it.

A couple of months after the Penydarren locomotive took to the rails for the first time, another important event occurred a short distance away. The Oystermouth Railway was incorporated by Act of Parliament on 29th June 1804 to carry passengers from Swansea, along the Gower Peninsula, to Mumbles. On 25th March 1807 it became the first railway in the world to carry fare-paying passengers. They were hauled by horses. Railway and steam engine were not to combine just yet.

In 1808 there were green fields in that part of London now occupied by the concrete jungle of University College, Bloomsbury. The curious observer though might have wondered about the circular wooden stockade that was being erected there. A handbill gave the answer, 'Trevithick's Portable Steam Engine,' it roared, 'Catch me who can. Mechanical Power Subduing Animal Speed.' Trevithick had invented the machine that one day would transform Britain, conquer the American West and open up Africa. And he put it in a sideshow.

For a time 'Captain Trevithick's dragon', as someone nicknamed it, was a fashionable attraction for Regency bucks and their ladies. It seems to have been an excellent little engine and deserved better than to trundle round in a circle all day. Eventually, like all fashions, the appeal of *Catch me who can* waned and soon afterwards Trevithick left for South America. There he made his fortune, lost it, and returned years later to die in poverty at a Dartford hotel.

Meanwhile the serious experimental work returned to the North of England. The Napoleonic Wars had forced up the price of animal fodder and economy-minded colliery owners were open to ideas, any ideas, about saving money. If steam locomotives were the answer, then so be it! The Middleton Railway has already played a significant part in this story; now it appears again. In 1812 Matthew Murray built the world's first commercially successful steam railway locomotive and ran it there.

Murray's engine was named *Salamanca*, after a recent battle in the Peninsular War when the Duke of Wellington had trounced Napoleon's forces. It too was a triumph in its way. *Salamanca* had features which were derived from and improved upon Trevithick's work, but it made use of a strange new rack and pinion system devised by John Blenkinsop. A cogwheel on the locomotive engaged special teeth in a rack on one side of the conventional rail. In terms of the evolution of today's railway it was a dead end. True the

(*Below*) A drawing depicting the scene on 27th September 1825, opening day on the Stockton & Darlington Railway. A horseman with a red flag rides ahead of Stephenson's engine No 1. *Locomotion* as it makes its historic way from Brusselton to Stockton.

(*Above*) Horses rode downhill in this Dandy Cart attached to the rear of a train of loaded wagons before pulling the empties back uphill. This method was used on the Stockton & Darlington.

locomotive could pull heavier loads because it gripped the rack tighter than a smooth wheel could grip a smooth rail, but rack and pinion would only ever be popular for mountain railways with their extremely steep gradients.

But Blenkinsop and Murray's system worked and they had the figures to prove it was more economical than using horses. People came from far and wide to view this phenomenon. Czar Nicholas of Russia was one; George Stephenson, engine-wright of Killingworth Colliery near Newcastle-upon-Tyne, was another.

George Stephenson, born at Wylam in 1781, was physically tough and mentally agile. Entirely self-taught, he had followed his father down the pit after first herding cows for 2d (1p) a day. At High Pit, Killingworth, he made a name for himself by servicing the newly acquired stationary pumping engine. His natural talent for things mechanical brought him to the attention of his superiors and by 1812 he was engine-wright earning £100 a year. Two years later and backed by Lord Ravensbourne, the owner of Killingworth Colliery, George Stephenson started building engines. His first,

Blucher (the name of the commander of the Prussian forces at the Battle of Waterloo), took to the rails in 1814.

Meanwhile at Wylam Colliery, close to Stephenson's birthplace, the manager, William Hedley, was building engines too. They were based on the locomotive bought from Trevithick which had been too heavy to use. The Hedley engines had vertical cylinders and resembled miniature beam engines on wheels. They were nicknamed *Grasshopper*, *Wylam Dilly* and *Puffing Billy*. The *Grasshopper* first steamed in May 1813 and because this was a good year before *Blucher's* appearance Hedley would argue forever afterwards that he, not Stephenson, was the true 'father of the railways'. He wasn't anything of the sort, of course.

Over the next five years Stephenson built a number of locomotives for both Killingworth and nearby Hetton collieries. He also endeavoured to tackle the problem that continued to spoil everything — rails were still too light and liable to crack under the weight of an engine. In 1820 rolled, or wrought, iron rails were produced for the first time and Stephenson adopted them enthusiastically. Now there were rails that could support any engine he built.

Finally all the development work came together because the merchants of Darlington wished 'for a more expeditious carriage of coals, lead, etc.' to the River Tees at Stockton. The Stockton & Darlington Railway received its Act of Parliament in 1821 and soon afterwards George Stephenson was appointed engineer. He quickly convinced the directors of the new company that steam engines should be used on the line.

What he couldn't do was find anyone from whom he could buy them. The answer was simple — build them himself. So in August 1823 the world's first railway locomotive builder was formed as Robert Stephenson & Company of the Forth Street Works, Newcastle-upon-Tyne. Robert was George's son and the workshops were to be in his charge.

The great day dawned, 27th September 1825, when the Stockton & Darlington Railway opened for business. Brass bands played, cannon boomed, and the crowds cheered as engine No. 1 *Locomotion* with George Stephenson himself at the controls steamed out of Brusselton, through Shildon and down to Stockton. *Locomotion's* train consisted mainly of waggons, some provided with planks to seat passengers on that special day only. Many more people sat upon the coal or sacks of flour in the other waggons. Among them however was a real purpose-built railway passenger coach called the *Experiment*. It meant that for the first time ever a steam locomotive hauled passengers on a public railway.

Led by a man on horseback and carrying a flag, the cavalcade soon reached 24 kph (15 mph) with its load of over 500 passengers. Later it kept pace with a stage-coach carrying only 16 people, in a convincing demonstration of 'mechnical power subduing animal speed'. The day was a resounding success; a railway had arrived. Not *the* railway though, for there were certain things about the Stockton & Darlington that still belonged to the past.

(*Above*) The original *Locomotion* enters Stockton in 1925 during the S & D R's centenary celebrations.

(*Below*) This full-scale working replica of *Locomotion* is kept at Beamish Open Air Museum.

On 10th October the *Experiment* began running every day except Sundays; it was pulled by horses. Steam, used with a flourish on opening day, stayed on the goods trains. Also the Stockton & Darlington was open for use by anyone who owned a waggon and a horse and wished to transport their goods along it themselves. This principle had been established when the Surrey Iron Railway, the world's first public goods line, was authorized back in 1801. In this sense early railways were no different from canals or turnpike roads which charged a toll or fee to everyone who used them.

The concept of a railway which ran only its own trains, to a strict timetable, on its own tracks had to wait just a few more years. The Stockton & Darlington was the halfway house of railway development. Part of it reflected the old-style waggonways of the past, while part looked to the new railway of the future. It was the end of the beginning.

2 The world's first inter-city line

Many toasts were drunk during the celebrations that marked the opening of the Stockton & Darlington Railway. One, the thirteenth, was to another new line which would soon connect Liverpool and Manchester. Few, if any, of the revellers realized as they raised their glasses that they were drinking the health of 48 km (30 miles) of railway that would shake the world. For in the Liverpool & Manchester project lay the real future of railways.

'King Cotton' was the boom industry of North West England, just as coal stamped its character on the face of the North East. In the 40 years from 1780 to 1820 production of cotton goods had increased twenty times over. India, the traditional supplier of raw cotton, had been supplanted by the southern states of America which sent their shipping to the port of Liverpool. From there the raw cotton went to the dark satanic mills of Manchester where it was refined and spun. Finally the finished product returned along the same route to be exported, again through Liverpool.

This constant flow of materials needed fast, efficient transport. In 1760 a canal system had been built by the Duke of Bridgewater to carry the goods; there were also roads of a sort with slow, lumbering stage-coaches to take businessmen who needed to travel between the two cities. As the amount of traffic in both goods and

(*Below*) A train of the Liverpool & Manchester Railway crosses Chat Moss bog, one of the line's engineering marvels.

Rocket, the winner of the Rainhill trials. This is a replica built in 1979.

> **TO ENGINEERS AND IRON FOUNDERS.**
>
> THE DIRECTORS of the LIVERPOOL and MAN-CHESTER RAILWAY hereby offer a Premium of £500 (over and above the cost price) for a LOCOMOTIVE ENGINE, which shall be a decided improvement on any hitherto constructed, subject to certain stipulations and conditions, a copy of which may be had at the Railway Office, or will be forwarded, as may be directed, on application for the same, if by letter, post paid.
>
> HENRY BOOTH, Treasurer.
>
> *Railway Office, Liverpool, April* 25, 1829.

The advertisement in the *Liverpool Mercury* of 1st May 1829 that announced the Rainhill trials.

passengers increased rapidly it became obvious that neither canal nor roads could cope. In winter both were often impassable because of ice or mud. It was said that a cargo which came from America in 21 days could lie on the dockside at Liverpool for as long as six weeks awaiting conveyance to Manchester. A railway was the obvious solution.

The idea had been around for quite some time by 1825 and at least one wealthy merchant had bankrupted himself promoting such a scheme. The Liverpool & Manchester Railway was destined to encounter other problems too. Only 160 km (100 miles) or thereabouts separates the North East from Lancashire, but in the 1820s — so far as railways were concerned — they were light years apart. By then there were enough short lines of one sort or another in the North East that local people took them for granted. Not so in Lancashire! There, railway engines were believed to be fearsome fire-belching machines that would terrify both people and horses, to say nothing of causing cows to stop giving milk!

During the initial surveys to plot a route for the new line, the Liverpool & Manchester Railway's surveyors faced considerable opposition. This came not only from ordinary people and farmers, who threw turnips or worse at them, but also from the wealthy landowners themselves. In the north it had often been the landowners who had promoted the railways to carry their coal; in Lancashire such men were frequently major shareholders in the canal. They faced financial disaster if the new-fangled railway took away its traffic.

George Stephenson, who was leading the survey team, wrote of two of his principal opponents: 'Bradshaw fires guns through his ground in the course of the night to prevent the surveyors coming on in the dark . . . Lord Sefton says he will have a hundred men against us.' Small wonder the surveyors hired a bare knuckle prize fighter to protect them!

Much preoccupied with the Stockton & Darlington, Stephenson's first survey of the Liverpool & Manchester route was skimpy. Important work was left to other, less-qualified, men. When the Bill for the new railway was presented before Parliament, the powerful landowners ganged together and employed brilliant lawyers to highlight its inaccuracies. Stephenson, who for all his engineering genius was basically an inarticulate man, made a poor show when giving evidence. The London lawyers mocked his thick Geordie accent and, worst of all, Stephenson himself knew many of their criticisms were right. The Bill was thrown out in 1825.

Another attempt was made at once. A fresh team of engineers, the Rennie brothers and a clever young army officer called Charles Vignoles, all excellent men, took over. New surveys were made and the line of route diverted away from the lands of the most vigorous opponents. This time things were done properly and the Bill for the Liverpool & Manchester Railway passed through Parliament without a hitch.

That was the easy bit; now the line had to be built. Straight and flat was the idea, but there were formidable obstacles. One was the 8 km (5 miles) wide Chat Moss, a spongy black bog that the locals said was bottomless. The broad Sankey Valley had to be crossed and a solid wall of rock barred the entry to Liverpool itself. Squabbles developed among the engineers which resulted in the Rennies and Vignoles eventually leaving the project. Stephenson left too, and then returned. He was on the threshold of his greatest triumph.

Never before had there been an engineering project like the Liverpool & Manchester Railway. It employed an army of travelling workmen to do magnificent feats with tools that were little more sophisticated than spades and pickaxes backed up by explosives. The men were called navvies, a name they inherited from the

Novelty built by Braithwaite and Ericcson was the popular favourite to win the Rainhill trials. It was fast but, in Stephenson's words, had no guts.

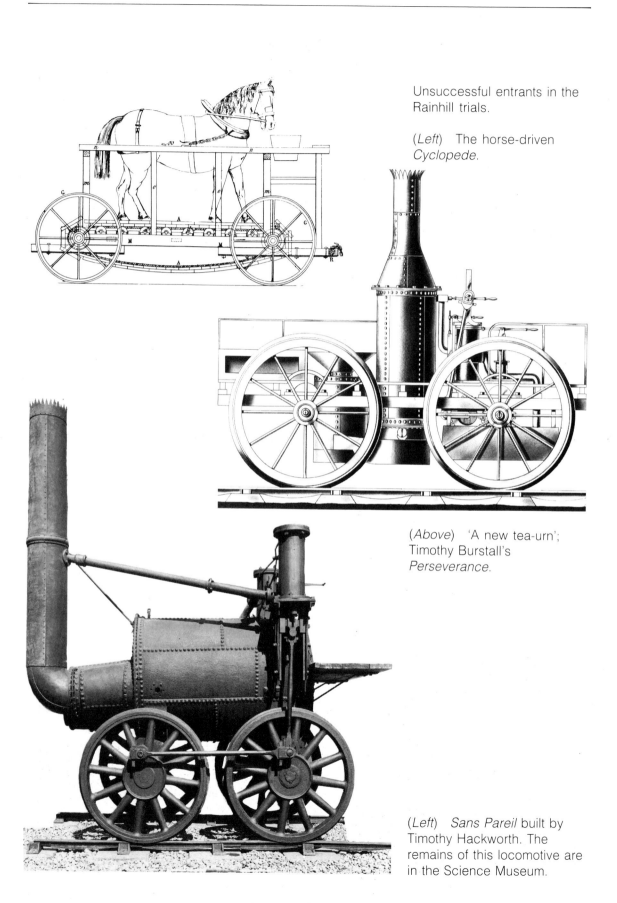

Unsuccessful entrants in the Rainhill trials.

(*Left*)   The horse-driven *Cyclopede*.

(*Above*)   'A new tea-urn'; Timothy Burstall's *Perseverance*.

(*Left*)   *Sans Pareil* built by Timothy Hackworth. The remains of this locomotive are in the Science Museum.

navigators who had cut out the canals during the previous century. Their muscle power poured tons of spoil, scrub, heather and brushwood into the inky depths of Chat Moss until finally, on New Year's Day 1830, it was possible to lay tracks across it.

Hundreds of navvies toiled away tunnelling and cutting the rock at the Liverpool end. Their methods were crude in the extreme. Shafts were sunk at intervals and then the men tunnelled horizontally in either direction. If the calculations were right then they all eventually joined up. At nearby Olive Mount a mighty chasm was blasted out of the rock and navvies hung by ropes on its bare sides as if mountaineering. A mighty nine-arch stone viaduct strode over the Sankey Valley and towered above the pigmy-like canal. As the barges passed below, their crews looked up in awe at the raw power of the railway that spelt doom for Britain's waterways.

By 1828 construction of the line was well advanced. But still no decision had been taken about which form of power would haul the trains. The directors of the Liverpool & Manchester had made one brief backward glance to the old days before abandoning any idea of allowing the railway to be open for all traffic on payment of a toll (like the Stockton & Darlington). Yet still they were not convinced that steam locomotives were the best power. Some directors preferred stationary engines placed at intervals along the line and hauling the trains by cable. Fifty-four would have been required, the cost immense and a single breakdown could paralyse the whole route.

The bargees look up in awe as the colossal Sankey Viaduct carries the railway confidently over the canal.

Stephenson, not surprisingly, championed the use of locomotives. Half-convinced, the directors sent out deputations to look at working railways. They went to the Middleton where Blenkinsop's rack and pinion line still functioned. At Shildon, on the Stockton & Darlington, Timothy Hackworth, the resident engineer, demonstrated his just-completed *Royal George*. With six-coupled wheels it was probably the most powerful engine in the country.

At last the directors reached a decision. There would be a great series of comparative locomotive trials over a 4 km (2½ mile) stretch of level track at Rainhill. The winning locomotive would be purchased for the Liverpool & Manchester line and its designer would receive £500 (worth £20,000 today). It was not a race. Conditions were set down which the engines had to meet, but they related to power, efficiency and economy rather than speed.

The Rainhill Trials commenced on 6th October 1829 and went on for over a week. Public interest was intense and every day a crowd of up to 15,000 spectators packed the specially erected grandstands as well as the fields on either side of the line. There were engineers and scientists from all over the world besides those who had come just to marvel at the wonder of the age.

Five engines were entered for the trials. Most famous of all, and the ultimate winner, was *Rocket* built by Robert Stephenson at Newcastle. Robert had been abroad for several years before returning to resume control of the Forth Street Works which had

(*Above*) A train passes through Olive Mount cutting outside Liverpool. This mighty chasm was hacked out by the muscle power of the navvies.

(*Right*) At Edge Hill, lines descended steeply down to the docks at Wapping and then on to Crown Street station. These sections were worked by ropes contained within the winding engines which were linked by a Moorish Arch.

declined in his absence. Now there was no stopping him. In South America he had met a fellow Englishman who was down on his luck; it was Richard Trevithick. They had talked about locomotives, and perhaps Robert had benefited from the older man's wisdom. *Rocket's* greatest advance, however, was the invention of Stephenson's assistant Henry Booth. It was a boiler with many small tubes to allow the fire through which vastly increased efficient steaming compared to the old system. Also *Rocket's* cylinders were not vertical as on other locomotives but set at an angle, and drove a single pair of large wheels with another smaller balancing pair behind.

Then there was *Sans Pareil* built by Timothy Hackworth (or 'Ackworth' as the official entry list misspelt his name). It was a massive locomotive but possessed no new features. Heavier than the specified limit for locomotives entering the trials, it was initially disqualified but later allowed to take part.

Novelty was entered by John Braithwaite and John Ericcson, a Swedish army officer. Living in London, they had heard about the competition only at the last moment and produced their locomotive in just seven weeks. Based on a road fire engine, *Novelty* presented a unique sight. 'A new tea urn', scoffed John Dixon, Stephenson's assistant, and not without reason.

The final two entrants were doomed to be also-rans from the very start. Timothy Burstall's *Perseverance* was hopelessly out of date and had been damaged when it fell from a road vehicle transporting

(*Above*) Inside Wapping Tunnel where the Liverpool & Manchester Railway burrowed its way into Liverpool's docks.

(*Below*) Opening day on the Liverpool & Manchester Railway, 15th September 1830. On the left is the Duke of Wellington's saloon.

it to Rainhill. *Cyclopede* entered by T Brandreth was even more bizarre than *Novelty*. It was basically a light cart containing a treadmill worked by two horses and mounted on rails.

In the event *Rocket* didn't quite have things all its own way. At the beginning of the trials *Novelty* quickly became the hero of the crowd. To their cheers it demonstrated a surprising turn of speed and raced along at an exhilarating 45 kph (28 mph). In an age when the fastest means of transport was the horse this brought excitement to fever pitch! 'It seemed to fly . . . it actually made me giddy to look at it,' wrote one observer. George Stephenson was astonished too, but is said to have summed up *Novelty* in two words, 'no guts'.

And so it proved. For it was *Rocket* alone that fulfilled all the conditions of the trial. The yellow and black engine hauled 12½ tons at a steady 19 kph (12 mph) and ran on its own at 24 to

(*Above*) A locomotive stops to take water at Parkside. This is where the unfortunate William Huskisson had his fatal accident.

(*Left*) George Stephenson's *Northumbrian*, which he drove on the opening day of the L & M R, hauling the train that carried the Duke of Wellington.

47 kph (15 to 29 mph). It then completed the all-important ten runs over the trial track, equal to the whole length from Liverpool & Manchester, hauling three times its own weight. *Perseverance* could manage only 10 kph (6 mph), *Cyclopede* even less, and both withdrew. *Sans Pareil* and *Novelty*, though made of sterner stuff, failed too with leaking joints and other problems. *Rocket*, it must be added, was frequently whisked up and down the track after one of these disasters as if to rub it in! The Stephensons had won a famous victory but now the line had to be completed.

On 15th September 1830, less than a year after Rainhill, the Liverpool & Manchester Railway was ready for its grand opening ceremony. This was to be an event of great national interest unlike the local celebrations for the Stockton & Darlington. The Duke of Wellington, Prime Minister 'Iron Duke' and hero of Waterloo, headed a host of VIPs from Britain and abroad who were to travel from Liverpool to Manchester that day. Not for them the waggons with planks used on the Stockton line's opening day. A 19 m (32 ft) long ornate ducal carriage decorated 'in the Grecian style' was provided, together with several scarcely less elegant vehicles, to accommodate the Duke's party.

The great cavalcade set off from Liverpool steaming majestically through the massive cutting at Olive Mount to the cheers of the multitude. Eight locomotives, all built by the Stephensons, ran in procession using both tracks. George Stephenson himself was driving *Northumbrian*, his latest engine and another significant

(*Above*)   *Planet* passes under the skew bridge at Rainhill.

(*Below*)   The line is open but navvies still hew rocks in Olive Mount Cutting. The men riding on the carriages are operating a type of primitive brake.

Liverpool and Manchester
RAIL-WAY.

TIME OF DEPARTURE
BOTH
From Liverpool & Manchester.

FIRST CLASS, FARE 5s. | SECOND CLASS, FARE 3s. 6d.

Seven o'Clock Morning. | *Eight o'Clock Morning.*
Ten   „   Do. | *Half-past Two Afternoon.*
One   „   Afternoon.
Half-past Four   Do.

*** For the convenience of Merchants and others, the First Class evening train of Carriages does not leave Manchester on *Tuesdays* and *Saturdays until Half-past Five o'Clock.*

The journey is usually accomplished by the First Class Carriages under two hours.

In addition to the above trains it is intended shortly to add three or four more departures daily.

The Company have commenced carrying GOODS of all kinds on the Rail-way.

January, 1831.

(*Above*) A grand new station was built at Lime Street, Liverpool, and opened in 1836. At first, trains were hauled up the steep incline to Edge Hill by ropes.

(*Above*) One of the world's first railway timetables, published only four months after the Liverpool & Manchester Railway had opened for business. The popularity of the new railway is indicated by the stated intention 'shortly to add three or four more departures daily'.

advance in design, which hauled the VIP carriages. It was a triumphant day. And it would end in tragedy.

At Parkside *Northumbrian* halted to take water. Despite a printed request that no one leave the train there, the distinguished guests got off and wandered about the tracks as if out for a stroll in Hyde Park. From his carriage the Duke of Wellington spotted the local Liverpool MP, William Huskisson, who had always been one of the most enthusiastic supporters of the Liverpool & Manchester. Although both were Tories they had quarrelled bitterly in the past. Railways in particular were something about which they disagreed for the Duke thought them a bad thing. 'They encourage the lower classes to travel about,' he had once said. But it was a day for putting aside old differences, and the Duke called to Huskisson, offering his hand in friendship.

Huskisson seemed pleased and crossed the track to the Duke's carriage. As he stood talking there was suddenly consternation among the party. An engine was bearing down upon them! There were wild shouts of warning as people scrambled out of the way.

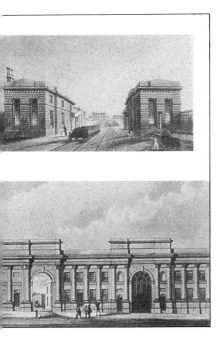

Poor Huskisson had recently been unwell and now seemed confused; he dithered in one direction and then another. Finally in desperation he clung to the open door of the Duke's carriage. *Rocket*, passing by at speed, hit the door, hurled Huskisson on to the tracks and ran over his leg. 'This is the death of me', murmured Huskisson, as he lay in agony upon the ground.

The badly injured man was placed gently on a flat car which had been emptied of its previous occupants, a brass band playing the procession on its joyful way. *Northumbrian* was attached and raced its sad cargo to nearby Eccles for medical help. With George Stephenson driving the locomotive was given its head and speed rose to a stagging 58 kph (36 mph). In any other circumstances this alone would have been cause for celebration. Alas, the mercy dash was in vain. Huskisson died a few hours later, the first passenger to be victim of a railway accident. The power of the railways and the impact of speed on a population geared to a slow rate of life had been fearfully demonstrated.

The day, 15th September 1830, which had begun in glory ended in disaster. When the great procession finally arrived at Manchester the Duke of Wellington was booed and jeered by the crowd who held him responsible for the 'Peterloo' massacre of demonstrators, eleven years previously. The waiting banquet was abandoned and it was a subdued and saddened party that returned through the darkness to Liverpool.

History allows us to see the true value of that day. The Liverpool & Manchester was quite simply the world's first real railway. It was purpose-built to carry both passengers and freight over a double track line of metal rails. Trains were steam-hauled throughout from the very beginning and ran to advertised timetables. In essence it was also the very first inter-city line. The long route from primitive early waggonway to modern railway was ended. The Liverpool & Manchester Railway had shown the future.

And it's still there today, now part of the InterCity network. Big diesels now race along at 90 mph over the route George Stephenson surveyed all those years ago. Surely he would approve.

3 Railway Mania

In 1830 there were less than 160 km (100 miles) of public railway in Great Britain. Twenty years later the total was 9,650 km (6,000 miles). This fury of building was known as the Railway Mania. The boom did not happen right away. After the opening of the Liverpool & Manchester Railway there was a pause. It was as if people stood back and marvelled at the new invention before its full potential hit them.

In fact the L&MR had not quite been the first public railway to use steam regularly to haul all their passengers. The Canterbury & Whitstable Railway had beaten them to this distinction by opening four months earlier in May 1830. But the C&WR was only a small local line and, like the others that followed in the next few years, was interested mainly in freight traffic. The Newcastle & Carlisle, opened in 1835, had even revived the stale old debate about whether or not to use steam locomotives, an argument that should have been dead and buried long ago. The success of steam on the L&MR had surely clinched things beyond any shadow of a doubt.

Then towards the end of the 1830s things began to change. In 1837 an eighteen-year-old girl called Alexandrina Victoria inherited the throne and there began a reign that would make Britain great. The brilliant achievements of the Victorian era would be built upon a solid foundation of industrial might supported by a superb railway system.

Now new much more ambitious routes were proposed. People rushed to invest their money in schemes that only a few years previously would have been thought crazy. Britain's first trunk, or long distance, line, the Grand Junction Railway, was opened in

The elegant station at King's Cross, built in 1852, which was the London terminus of the Great Northern Railway. Today, InterCity 125 High Speed Trains use its platforms.

1837. It connected the important industrial centre of Birmingham with the Liverpool & Manchester Railway. At the same time Robert Stephenson, no longer just a builder of locomotives but now a great engineer like his father, was building the London & Birmingham Railway. A great grecian-style Doric arch marked the entrance to its southern terminus at Euston, only a few hundred metres from the site where Trevithick's *Catch me who can* had chuffed away its short life. When the London & Birmingham was completed it linked with the Grand Junction and that met with the Liverpool & Manchester. Now there were the beginnings of a real railway system.

Confidence seized the railway builders and it was echoed by the whole country. Suddenly it seemed as if every town and city wanted its own railway. George Stephenson had always held a vision of a great nationwide railway network. And perhaps without even realizing it he was responsible for one thing which made it so much easier to achieve. Track gauge is the width between the two parallel rails on a section of line. The amount of space between the wheels of locomotives and carriages has to be identical for them to run on it. If all the new lines were eventually to join up and make a unified system then the gauge of each individual railway had to be the same.

The gauge of the old waggonways varied. It seems likely that the rails were set down just far enough apart to take the existing horse-drawn vehicles. At Killingworth Colliery, where George Stephenson built his first locomotives, the track gauge was 1,435 mm (4 ft 8½ ins.), so naturally he built them to fit this dimension. When he

(*Left*) The Newcastle & Carlisle Railway, opened in sections between 1835 and 1838, was the first line across England. This train, with its assortment of carriages conveying both people and animals, is running beside the River Tyne at Wylam.

(*Below*) The great Doric arch which marked the entrance to the London & Birmingham Railway's southern terminus at Euston. Built in 1838, the arch was demolished when the new Euston station was constructed in the 1960s.

later became engineer to the Stockton & Darlington Railway, and also builder of its locomotives, he not surprisingly constructed both track and engines to this same gauge.

George Stephenson also acted as advisor to the Canterbury & Whitstable and Leicester & Swannington railways; he built the Liverpool & Manchester. All used Stephenson-built engines, all had a track gauge of 1,435 mm (4 ft 8½ ins.) His son Robert used the same gauge for his two greatest projects, the London & Birmingham Railway and the Chester & Holyhead Railway. So did Joseph Locke, who had worked with the Stephensons on the L&MR, when he built the Grand Junction Railway.

The advantages of having all Britain's railways to the same gauge were obvious, but one great pioneer railway builder went his own way. This was Isambard Kingdom Brunel, a small man with a giant reputation, and engineer to the infant Great Western Railway. He was convinced that a mighty 'broad gauge' of 2,140 mm (7 ft 0¼ in) would make for a safer, smoother and faster ride. In many ways he was right, but it was already too late. In 1844 the government's Royal Commission on Gauges decided in favour of a standard gauge which would have to be used, by law, on all new railways – it was 1,435 mm. Stephenson had got in first.

Existing projects that were already under construction using a different gauge could continue, however. Brunel was masterminding the GWR and several other railways in the West Country that were

(*Above*) The engineering works on the L & B R surpassed anything that had gone before. This is the Hampstead Road Bridge.

(*Above*) The great ventilating shaft in Kilsby tunnel near Rugby.

(*Right*) The entrance to the locomotive depot at Camden Town.

designed to take the broad gauge from Paddington to Penzance. He carried on, but he continued alone. Soon, 'break of gauge' occurred at junction stations where the lines of standard-gauge railways met the GWR. The standard-gauge trains could not go any further or vice versa. It meant passengers and freight had laboriously to be transferred between the two types of trains, a procedure which was messy, inconvenient and awkward.

Brunel was a truly great engineer, indeed he was a genius; and his broad gauge was a great engineering feat. But he lacked the commercial vision to see the GWR as part of national railway network and viewed it only in isolation. Eventually his beloved broad gauge was complete. It swept from smoky London to the golden sands and salt sea spray of Western Cornwall, almost to Land's End itself. The wide gleaming rails plunged into the inky depths of Box Tunnel in Wiltshire, where it was said the sun's rays penetrated only on one day each year, and that was 9th April — Brunel's birthday. They were carried high over the tall-masted warships on the River Tamar by Brunel's stupendous Royal Albert Bridge that linked Devon to Cornwall. The broad gauge was magnificent. But gradually the inconvenience outweighed the spectacle. The GWR built its new lines to the standard gauge or turned the broad-gauge lines into mixed gauge by adding an extra rail between the existing two. Mixed gauge meant that trains of both gauges could operate over the same route. Slowly the broad-gauge empire shrank. Then during a single weekend in May 1892 an army of workmen tore up the last of the broad-gauge rails to end Brunel's great dream.

With the coming of the railways, it was soon obvious that people actually wanted to travel just for the fun of it. Previously a man might never in his whole lifetime have walked beyond the outskirts of his own village. Now he wanted to see what was over the horizon.

London & Birmingham RAILWAY.

ON AND AFTER MONDAY, THE 11th OF JUNE,

AN ADDITIONAL

TRAIN

BETWEEN

RUGBY

AND

BIRMINGHAM,

Will Commence Running.

(SUNDAYS EXCEPTED)

TO LEAVE RUGBY AT 9 A.M., AND TO RETURN FROM BIRMINGHAM AT 6 P.M.,

Stopping at Coventry to take up & set down Passengers.

RICHARD CREED, } Secretaries of
C. R. MOORSOM, } the Board.

Birmingham, June 7, 1838.

(*Above*) Traffic on the increase. The London & Birmingham was the first main line into London and was completed on 17th September 1838.

In many ways the old stage-coaches had done a good job and in some areas provided a relatively frequent service. But there just weren't enough of them. The stage-coaches which ran between Leeds and Bradford could carry only eleven passengers, which meant that no more than 180 people could be conveyed between the two great cities in a single day. During the summer of 1835 the newly opened Leeds & Selby Railway carried over 3,500 passengers each week compared to the mere 400 who had been able to use stage-coaches on the same route. 'Railroad travelling is a delightful improvement of human life,' wrote one enthusiast in 1842. 'The early Scotchman scratches himself in the morning mists of the North and has his porridge in Piccadilly before the setting sun. Everything is near, . . . time, distance and delay are abolished.'

The dramatic growth in passenger traffic astounded the directors of the early lines. The Liverpool & Manchester was soon cancelling the freight trains for which it had primarily been built and running extra passenger services instead. To cater for the public's desire to travel for travel's sake the excursion train was introduced. These

London and Birmingham Railway.

[734]

FREE TICKET.—SECOND CLASS.

DEPARTMENT.

No. *4 5* Train *1840.*

From *Watford* to *Tring*

Name *J Jackson*

Why granted *on business*

Head of Department.

N.B. Free Tickets are granted to persons employed on the Company's Business only, and must be given up when demanded.

DOWN.

(*Right*) A free ticket to travel between Watford and Tring. It is made of paper, not card, and is mainly handwritten.

(*Above*) The first train ran over the broad gauge Great Western Railway on 4th June 1838. This is a re-enactment 100 years later.

The western approach to the GWR's Box Tunnel. It is believed Brunel designed this tunnel so that the sun would shine through on his birthday.

were special trains run to take people to a particular event; they offered low fares and were enormously popular right from the start.

The first excursion train was organized by the Mechanics' Institute in Nottingham and ran from there to Leicester on 20th July 1840. Soon afterwards another excursion on the Midland Counties Railway was described by an onlooker as; 'perhaps the longest train ever known . . . it had four engines to drag it along and appeared like a moving street.'

Excursion trains were big business and their fame spread. In North Cornwall the Bodmin & Wadebridge Railway arranged an outing to see a public hanging at Bodmin Gaol! Three trains were run and as the B&W was a freight line with only four coaches passengers travelled in wagons built to carry sea-sand. Conveniently the wharf siding at Bodmin was right next to the gaol so no one had to leave their seats while the Lightfoot brothers were executed.

At the opening of each new railway there were great celebrations. Brass bands played, banquets were held and important speeches made. In the North East, ox-roasting was a popular part of the festivities. When the South Devon Railway opened its line to Paignton in 1839 there was a riot during the sharing-out of a huge pudding weighing one-and-a-half tons!

The zenith of the Railway Mania was in 1846 when 272 Acts of Parliament were passed authorizing new railways. Almost 6,500 km (4,000 miles) were opened between then and 1850. George Hudson, a draper from York, became known as the 'Railway King' because

(*Left*) Carrying more trains than anyone could have imagined when it was built in 1840, the Ouse Viaduct is still part of the London to Brighton main line.

(*Above*) The first American-designed locomotives to run in Britain were some 4–2–0s built by Norris & Co. of Philadelphia in 1840 for the Birmingham & Gloucester Railway's Lickey Incline.

A Liverpool & Manchester Railway engine of 1835.

of his wheeler-dealing in railway shares. He bought up lots of small companies and made a fortune, but eventually he was discovered to be acting fraudulently and his empire crashed about his ears. George Hudson did one good thing, however, which set an example soon to be copied everywhere. In 1844 he amalgamated three small lines into one larger company, the Midland Railway. It was the way ahead.

Two years later, in 1846, the London & Birmingham joined with both the Manchester & Birmingham and the Grand Junction Railway, which had already swallowed up the old Liverpool & Manchester line. Together they formed the mighty London & North Western Railway with a vast network of lines stretching from London to the Midlands and North West, England's industrial heartland. Within a year the LNWR took over the Lancaster & Carlisle Railway. Then in 1848 it reached an agreement with the Caledonian Railway to run through trains from London over its tracks from Carlisle to Glasgow. A mere 20 years previously it had taken well over 40 hours to travel from London to Scotland, now it could be done in less than a day.

But soon the Euston to Glasgow line, known as the West Coast route, was not the only way of getting from London to Scotland. By 1852 there was an East Coast route to Edinburgh, via York and Newcastle, and its London terminus was at King's Cross, less than half a mile from Euston. The rivalry between these two routes was to smoulder on with occasional outbreaks of open warfare for over a century.

(*Right*) An invitation to the opening of the Kendal & Windermere Railway on 20th April 1847.

(*Right*) Railway progress was rapid in the 1840s. Here a train of the Liverpool & Bury Railway crosses the London & North Western in 1849.

(*Below*) *Lion* was built for the Liverpool & Manchester Railway by the firm of Todd, Kitson & Laird in 1838. It is now preserved and is the oldest engine in Britain capable of being steamed. The coaches seen here are replicas from the National Railway Museum.

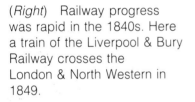

New lines were being built at a tremendous rate and sometimes there were head-on conflicts as the newcomers sought Parliamentary powers to run over the tracks of existing companies. Many stations became jointly-owned or used by more than one company's trains. The older railways often did not take too kindly to intruders muscling in on their patch and occasionally there were pitched battles as they tried to prevent them.

At Chester station in 1849 the LNWR staff ejected the Shrewsbury & Chester Railway's booking clerk from his office and threw his tickets after him! When the first Shrewsbury & Birmingham Railway train attempted to run over the LNWR in 1851 it was fiercely opposed. Engines of the two railways met head-on like fighting bulls to the cheers of an army of police, troops and hundreds of sightseers. The Great Northern Railway were involved in trouble when they first ran a train into the Midland Railway station at Nottingham. A posse of Midland locomotives were sent to hem in the GNR engine and forced it away to a disused shed. The rails were then pulled up and the unfortunate locomotive remained there for seven months!

But these were minor hiccups in a relentless advance, for by 1850 the national railway network in which George Stephenson had believed was well underway. And in its wake the character of the British people began to change. As the effects of distance were destroyed by the speed of railway travel, people developed a feeling of belonging to one nation rather than just their local community. Once it had taken days for news of great events to reach the countryside, now newspapers could be distributed in just a few hours. Mail was first conveyed by rail on the Liverpool & Manchester Railway on 11th November 1830. Soon afterwards special carriages in which the letters could be sorted while on the move were introduced on the Grand Junction Railway.

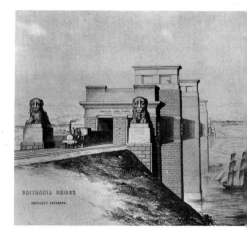

(*Above*)   Designed by Robert Stephenson, the Britannia Bridge was opened in March 1850.

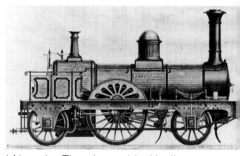

(*Above*)   The *Jenny Lind* built in 1847.

(*Below*)   Opened a year before the Britannia Bridge, the Conway Tubular Bridge was also built by Robert Stephenson. The towers were designed to blend in with Conway Castle nearby.

A contrast in 'single wheelers'. (*Left*) Stephenson's 'long boiler' engine.

(*Below*) No. 2002 of the Bristol & Exeter Railway. The massive driving wheels were 2.7m (8' 10") in diameter. They were extremely fast engines and one reached a speed of 131.6 kph (81.8 mph) in June 1854.

Not only news travelled faster. By 1848 the Eastern Counties Railway was bringing 70 tons of fish to London each week. In those pre-freezer days fish had been eaten mainly by people who lived close to the sea. Now the railways could whisk it across the country before it had a chance to go bad. Thanks to the railways fish and chips became a popular meal.

Time itself altered with the coming of the railways. For centuries country people had based their lives on local time which differed by up to several minutes from Greenwich Mean Time. The need to run all trains to a common timetable, whether at one end of the country or the other, meant GMT had to be used everywhere. 'Railway Time' set the standard throughout the country.

As the number of adjoining railways increased, it became possible for passengers and freight to travel on journeys over the tracks of

more than one company. To divide up the money from these through journeys the Railway Clearing House was set up with hundreds of clerks to sort out the paperwork. In 1836 Thomas Edmondson, a booking clerk on the Newcastle & Carlisle Railway, had invented a ready-printed cardboard railway ticket. It was a considerable saving in effort and time from the previous hand-written tickets and only now, 150 years later, is it being replaced by computer-printed tickets.

While the network of lines was expanding like a giant spider's web across the face of Britain, the trains were changing too. After *Rocket*, locomotive development was rapid and new engines began to take on a familiar appearance. A typical locomotive of the 1840s had the boiler, smokebox and firebox set on a frame which also supported the wheels. The previous, very precarious, perch for driver and fireman had widened into a proper footplate but as yet no engine had a cab to protect them from the bad weather. No wonder most Victorian enginemen wore beards! Cylinders were usually mounted horizontally under the frame and powered a pair of large driving wheels. Two more pairs of free-running wheels were placed under the engine in front of and behind the driving wheels. The arrangement was classed as the 2-2-2 type by counting the number of wheels in each group.

This type of 'single-wheeler', as it was known, was built first by Robert Stephenson in 1833 and quickly copied by others. One such engine, called *Lucifer*, on the Grand Junction Railway reached a speed of 91 kph (56¾ mph) on 13th November 1839. Later speed records were set up the Great Western Railway, justifying Brunel's belief in the possibilities for fast running on his broad gauge. His 2-2-2 *Great Western* hit 120 kph (74½ mph) at Wootton Bassett on 1st June 1846, and two years later *Great Britain* was pushed up to a top speed of 125.5 kph (78 mph) at the same place. This was more than twice the highest speed achieved by *Rocket* only fifteen years before. Man had never travelled so fast. By 1850 the railways of Britain had over 2,500 locomotives — all steam of course!

Improvements to passenger accommodation unfortunately were

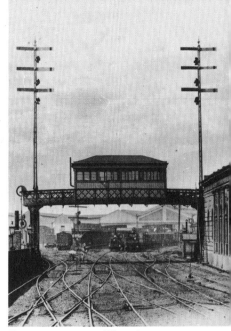

The entrance to Waterloo station, London & South Western Railway, in 1868. The signalbox is set above the tracks.

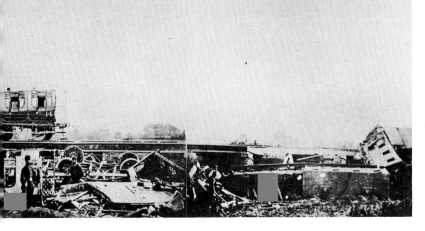

(*Left*) On 9th June 1865 the South Eastern Railway's Folkestone Boat Express crashed at Staplehurst in Kent. Charles Dickens was among the passengers and was badly shaken. He died exactly five years later.

not so speedy. In a society that believed everyone should know their place, the coming of mass travel by train presented a problem. How could the lower orders be kept apart from their betters? Simple: just carry the class system through to railway carriages. From the day it opened the Liverpool & Manchester had three types of accommodation, all at varying fares. First-class carriages were based on horse carriage design and resembled three stage-coach bodies joined together. Each body was separate from the other and this is the origin of the non-corridor compartment coaches still found occasionally today. The interiors were quite luxurious with padded seats. Second class was much the same externally but with wooden seating inside. Third-class carriages, however, were little more than goods wagons with benches fitted to them. They had no roofs and holes were drilled in the floors to allow the rainwater to run away.

From the beginning railway companies preferred to carry only the more profitable first and second class passengers, but the Regulation of Railways Act in 1844 forced them to run at least one train conveying third class passengers each day over every line on their

(*Above*) The staff of the locomotive department at Derby on the Midland Railway about 1860. They are posing in front of an 0–6–0 goods engine designed by Matthew Kirtley.

(*Below*) Somerset & Dorset Railway 2–4–0 No. 2, built in 1861. Note the primitive cab.

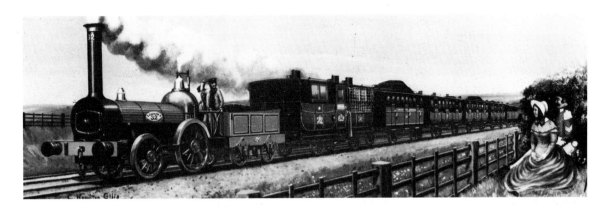

system stopping at all stations. Speeds were not to be less than 19 kph (12 mph) and fares were fixed at 1d (½p) a mile. This was done most grudgingly and for many years afterwards any slow local train was nicknamed the 'Parly' (Parliamentary) by staff.

The 1844 act also stipulated that third class passengers should be carried in covered accommodation. Again this was done in poor spirit by the railways and little comfort was offered inside these new cell-like carriages. Train lighting was provided by means of individual oil lamps. There were several in each first and second class carriage, one in third class. There were no heating and no toilets; you needed to be tough to travel by train in the 1840s. There were also no continuous brakes. Brakes were fitted to the locomotives and a few individual carriages in each train. Brakesmen sat high above the ends of these coaches in an exposed and dangerous position ready to apply the brakes by hand as required.

Great civil engineering works stamped their mark upon the countryside as the iron rails marched relentlessly on. The scenes of construction on a grand scale that had characterized the building of the Liverpool & Manchester Railway were now repeated everywhere. Mighty viaducts, bridges, cuttings, embankments and tunnels took the railways across the length and breadth of Britain. Still with only relatively primitive equipment, tens of thousands of navvies toiled and sweated to give the country a solidly-built system that has stood the test of time — unlike the motorways of recent years. No longer did the engineers feel the need to plan their

(*Above*) Travelling on the London & Birmingham Railway in 1845. The leading vehicle is a travelling post office in which mail was sorted while on the move.

(*Below*) In 1833 the Leicester & Swannington's engine *Samson* ran into a horse and cart which was crossing the tracks. Asked to find a method of giving warning of a train's approach George Stephenson devised a 'steam trumpet' which was fitted to *Samson* and operated by steam from the boiler. It was the world's first locomotive whistle.

(*Above*) Railway mania was intense during the 1840s but it never reached the heights (or depths) suggested by this cartoon.

(*Above*) No. 25 *Derwent* built by the Stockton & Darlington Railway in 1845. It was primitive in appearance compared to new locomotives elsewhere at that time.

railways along a flat and straight path. There was no natural obstacle they could not overcome. Less than a decade after Rainhill, Joseph Locke had put a railway over the bleak hills of Shap Fell between Lancaster and Carlisle. The gradients were ferocious: the climb to Shap would remain a test of enginemen's skill and the power of their locomotives until the end of steam.

Less impressive was the development of signalling equipment. The early railway companies seem to have vaguely imagined that a force similar to the newly-created civil police would look after train control between their other duties. To this day train drivers sometimes refer to the signalman as 'bobby'. A railway police force was introduced but its responsibilities soon lay elsewhere. At first a simple time interval was allowed between trains, but as traffic increased it became obvious that something safer was required.

An assortment of fixed signals was devised, culminating in the semaphore type introduced on the London & Croydon Railway in 1841. A moveable wooden signal arm was slotted into the top of a tall post and controlled by a lever at its foot. Gradually the block system was developed. Each line was divided into sections at the beginning of which there was a semaphore signal. Another new invention, the electric telegraph, was used to send simple messages from one signalman to the next. When a train arrived at the first signal it was put to clear, usually by lowering the arm, and the train allowed to travel on to the next section of line. The signalman then sent a message to his colleague at the next signal to say the train was on its way. After it had arrived, the second signalman sent a message back to the first to say that the train was out of his section of line. This meant another train could now be allowed in. The block system was primitive and took a long while to gain popularity. Many lines still preferred to rely on the time interval method. But it had the beginnings of today's electronic signalling systems that make travel by train so safe.

The track itself also improved a little during the 1840s and 1850s. Rails had originally been laid on stone blocks, but slowly the use of wooden sleepers placed at right angles became more widespread. Brunel, ever an individualist, used wooden sleepers but put them lengthways under the rails.

In the summer of 1859 a sad convoy made its way over the magnificent Royal Albert Bridge at Saltash, just west of Plymouth. Steaming gently it passed under the giant tubular arches that strode so confidently over the River Tamar. When, only weeks previously, Prince Albert, Victoria's Consort, had opened the bridge the crowds had roared their approval. Brunel's great broad gauge route to the West was complete. But today there were no crowds, no flags, no brass bands to play as a lone engine chuffed slowly over the bridge. Brunel himself lay propped on pillows in an open wagon behind the locomotive. He was dying and this was to be the only time he would see his completed masterpiece.

By the autumn of 1859 Brunel was dead. Within a year both Robert Stephenson and Joseph Locke too had died. With the passing of these pioneers, all of them giants of the engineering world, went a link with the first days of the railways. The foundations of Britain's great railway network were complete.

'THE DEPARTURE – THIRD CLASS' (*Above*) and 'THE RETURN – FIRST CLASS' (*Below*). A pair of Victorian paintings showing typical carriage interiors of the 1850s.

4 Railway age

If, by some miracle, a time machine could take us back to Carlisle station as it was in 1900, the sight before us would be truly magnificent. For this was the heyday of Britain's independent railway companies. By the turn of the century there were more than 130 different and highly individualistic railways. And, at Carlisle's great Citadel station, it was possible to see the trains of no less than seven of them. Here the shining blackberry-black engines of the London & North Western Railway handed over the Anglo-Scottish expresses to the Prussian blue locomotives of the Caledonian Railway (a few years later the Caley would paint their crack engines sky blue to give an even more spectacular appearance). A rival line to Scotland brought in the rich red engines of the Midland Railway. If the Midland train's final destination was Glasgow then mid-green Glasgow & South Western Railway locomotives took over; if it was Edinburgh, one (or two) of the unusual brownish-green liveried engines of the North British Railway would couple on.

These were only the main lines; two other, secondary, lines entered Carlisle. Round the western coast came the little Maryport & Carlisle with its ancient green engines and stubby elderly coaches. Small tunnels on the route meant all their rolling stock had to be narrower than normal. From Newcastle in the east, a cross-country line owned by one of the railway giants also entered Carlisle. The North Eastern Railway had long ago swallowed up the pioneer Stockton & Darlington line, but its finances too were firmly bedded in the coal-rich counties of Durham and Northumberland. NER locomotives were green also, but a brighter shade than any of the others.

The carriages of the seven companies were a paint box of colour as well: purplish-brown and white (LNWR); brownish-red (CR); plum red (NER); purplish-red (NBR); crimson lake (MR and GSWR) and green and cream (Maryport & Carlisle). As the trains steamed in and out of Carlisle there was a constant kaleidoscope of colour.

Fit for a Queen. In 1897 the Great Western Railway built a new royal train for Victoria's Diamond Jubilee. At its head is 4–2–2 No. 3041, until recently called *Emlyn*, now renamed *The Queen*. There is a crown on the engine's headlamp and gigantic cast-iron mouldings of the royal arms on both sides of locomotive and tender. Railway Regalia!

This high spot of Britain's steam railways coincided with the zenith of its Empire. Three years previously Queen Victoria herself had travelled through Carlisle in the Royal Train. She was heading north to Balmoral after the Diamond Jubilee celebrations in London that had marked 60 glorious years of her reign. The party spirit had entered even the LNWR. Abandoning their usual black livery they had repainted No. 2053 *Greater Britain* in bright post office red to work the Euston to Crewe section of her journey. There it was replaced by No. 2054 *Queen Empress*, decked out in white to speed like a ghost through the darkness. At Carlisle the Caledonian's blue engines took over to complete a patriotic red, white and blue colour sequence. Sadly, history does not tell us if the old Queen, who was doubtless tired by all the festivities in London, ever noticed this unique tribute.

Victoria had been an early champion of the railways. On 13th June 1842 she became the first reigning British monarch to travel by train when she journeyed from Slough to Paddington on the infant Great Western Railway. This was over Brunel's broad gauge and he rode upon the engine himself accompanying Daniel Gooch, the GWR's Locomotive Superintendent, who was driving. The

(*Above*) The GWR's broad gauge engines were a magnificent sight. This is *Lord of the Isles* built in 1851. It was preserved for some years but scrapped in 1906.

(*Above*) End of an era: workmen converting broad gauge tracks to standard gauge.

(*Left*) Only hours before, on 20th May 1892, the last broad gauge express had swept through Sonning Cutting, near Reading, behind 4–2–2 *Bulkeley*. Here the track is mixed with both broad and standard gauge rails in place.

(*Left*) Redundant broad gauge carriages awaiting breaking up at Swindon works.

(*Above*) Queen Victoria and her growing family take the train.

engine was exotically named *Phlegethon* after a fiery river in hell. High-minded Victorians loved classical names for their locomotives. Many faint hearts had warned the Queen of the probable dreadful consequences of travelling by this strange new method of transport, but she came to no harm. Later, Victoria wrote that she was 'quite charmed' by the experience. For the rest of her long life she would be a frequent, if sometimes awkward, traveller by rail. She didn't like to go too fast, wouldn't eat on the train and hated any change to her surroundings. As her family expanded so did the railway network. Victoria had residences at opposite ends of the country: Osborne on the Isle of Wight and Balmoral near Aberdeen. This, and her many state visits, meant that her railway journeys soon became widespread.

From the very beginning the bigger companies had each built a complete Royal Train just for Victoria and her entourage. 'Palaces on Wheels' is the only description for these luxurious carriages with their interiors of deep velvet, shimmering silk and gleaming brass. Whenever possible only the newest locomotives were selected to work a Royal Train. Before taking up its duties, a royal engine would be highly polished and the coal in the tender whitewashed. Decorative bunting would be twisted around the handrails and perhaps a massive coloured cast iron representation of the Royal Coat of Arms placed in front of the smokebox. Railway regalia indeed.

This sort of patriotic extravagance continued even after Victoria's death. In 1911 the suburban London, Tilbury & Southend Railway marked the Coronation of King George V by adorning its 4-4-2 tank engine No. 80 *Thundersley* (named after a village in Essex). First it was almost buried beneath garlands of flowers strung about the

(*Above*) Her Majesty's day compartment in the London and North Western Railway royal train. This postcard was one of millions sold by the LNWR.

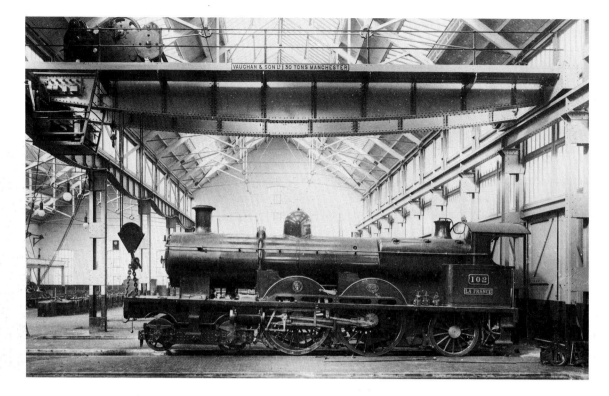

tanks. Then plaster busts of both King and Queen were crowded on to the engine's front buffer beam. And this wasn't for any Royal Train. *Thundersley* ran in normal service conveying startled commuters to and from their homes in East London and Essex.

In later years Royal Trains, though still elegant, became more plainly furnished. Even today our present Queen continues the fashion set by her great-great-grandmother and travels extensively in her own special train. Today's royal saloons can do 100 mph. Queen Victoria would not have been amused!

The railway network now extended over almost the whole of Great Britain. It was estimated that by 1914 no village in England was more than 32 km (20 miles) from the nearest station. After the basic system of main lines had been all but completed in the 1850s and 1860s there was a slight slackening off in new construction. There were 21,700 km (13,500 miles) of route on the railway map

Only a very few foreign-built locomotives have ever run on Britain's railways.

(*Above*) *La France* was imported by the GWR in 1903 so that engineer Churchward could study its system of re-using exhaust steam, known as compounding. It was a complicated machine and, after taking it to bits, Churchward exclaimed 'this is watchmaker's work'.

(*Left*) There was a great locomotive shortage around 1900 when every railway works in Britain was full to capacity. Three companies turned to America for new locomotives. This is Midland Railway No. 2506, a 2–6–0 built by Baldwins of Philadelphia and a typical American design of the period. These engines were very roughly made.

of 1870 and 30,000 km (18,665 miles) by 1900. Twelve years later the total had grown to 32,265 km (20,053 miles). The lines that were built during these forty years took the railway to the remoter parts of North Devon, Cornwall, Norfolk, the Isle of Wight and the Scottish Highlands.

Many of these new lines never stood a chance of carrying enough traffic to make a profit. Some were built by one company to deny a rival access to a particular town, others had no purpose but to compete with existing routes. For six years the Midland Railway, egged-on by its partner companies, struggled to build the Settle to Carlisle line over some of the bleakest, most inhospitable territory in England. Shanty towns housed the hundreds of navvies who worked in all weathers to hew out the line across the high fells on

(*Above*) GWR 4–4–0 No. 3440 *City of Truro*, the first locomotive in Britain to reach 160 kph (100 mph). It is now preserved.

(*Below*) GWR 4–6–2 No. 111 *The Great Bear* built in 1908 was the first Pacific to run in this country. Not a success, it was rebuilt as a 4–6–0 in 1924 and renamed *Viscount Churchill*.

(*Above*) The great signal gantry that guarded the southern approach to Rugby.

(*Above*) Lyme Regis terminus. The engine is a second-hand 'terrier' tank bought from the London, Brighton & South Coast Railway. The London & South Western Railway's Axminster to Lyme Regis branch opened on 24th August 1903.

(*Right*) Cannington viaduct, the line's most impressive structure, under construction.

the backbone of England. It was a magnificent achievement and meant the Midland had its own line to Carlisle and beyond. But there were already two other competing routes to Scotland.

Cross-country lines meandered through the backwaters of Britain. Many were jointly owned by two different companies so that each could run its carriages through to places far from their usual routes. The Somerset & Dorset Joint Railway (nicknamed the 'slow and dirty' or 'swift and delightful' depending on your experience of it) was operated by the Midland Railway and the London & South Western Railway. Its existence allowed the Midland to send trains direct to Bournemouth from Sheffield, Derby or Nottingham.

Branch lines were laid to serve villages off the main lines. The branch train was often where ageing engines and musty, elderly coaches eked out their final days, like old horses put out to grass. For the really remote country districts 'light railways' were authorized by Act of Parliament. These ramshackle affairs were permitted to run a very shoestring operation so long as they observed basic safety rules. Narrow gauge lines also served places way off the railway map — there was one on the Mull of Kintyre, in Scotland, for instance.

As we have seen already, each of the independent railways favoured different, highly distinctive liveries for their locomotives and rolling stock. The engines themselves were different too. As their empires grew the biggest companies increasingly turned away from the private locomotive building firms such as Robert Stephenson had pioneered at Newcastle in 1823. They established their own workshops to construct engines, carriages and wagons. Repair shops were set up too. Whole railway towns grew up around these works, the men living in housing owned and provided by the company. Swindon on the Great Western and Crewe on the Grand Junction (later London & North Western) scarcely existed before they were picked to be the engineering centres of their respective railways.

The private locomotive builders flourished as well. Smaller railways could not afford their own workshops and brought 'off the peg'. The big companies frequently did not have enough space to

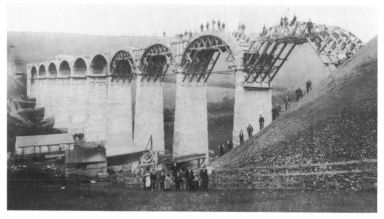

(*Left*) The Forth Bridge, north of Edinburgh, took eight years to build and was completed in 1890. It is 2.528 kilometres (1 mile and 1,005 yards) long.

construct all the locomotives they needed, and so turned back to outside industry. Britain became the railway workshop of the world, and locomotives left these shores for the remotest parts of Africa, South America, India and Asia.

Today it is called corporate identity — the unique appearance of a particular firm or its products that distinguishes it from its rivals. All the old railways had it, to a greater or lesser degree. It extended from the buttons on staff uniforms to the building style of its stations and signalboxes. Stations, big and small, varied greatly in their architecture. Just stand in London's Euston Road and contrast the elegant simplicity of King's Cross with the fairy-tale castle-like riot of turrets and spires that is St Pancras. They are separated by only a few metres in distance and less than 20 years in time (St Pancras being the later of the two), but are a world apart in architectural style. As Britain's railway network increased so did its industrial wealth. In the major manufacturing cities stations were as grand and imposing as any other of the new civic buildings, the town hall for instance. By the end of the nineteenth century the volume of traffic at many stations had far outstripped the original modest facilities. New, grander and more spacious buildings were erected to take their place.

Large country stations sometimes imitated manor houses from

(*Above*) St Pancras station in 1876. The buildings in front of the station were actually the Midland Railway's Grand Hotel and are now offices.

(*Below*) Ribblehead viaduct on the Settle to Carlisle line took five years to build.

(*Above*) The station at Waterloo, London & South Western Railway, in the early 1900s before rebuilding.

(*Above*) A 1913 view of Manchester, London Road station, owned jointly by the London & North Western and Great Central Railways. It was replaced by the new Piccadilly station in the 1960s. (*Right*) Yeovil in 1911, a typical large country junction station. The centre tracks were for expresses to pass through without stopping.

Tudor or Jacobean times. Tiny branch line buildings would be made of warm local brick or mellow stone, to melt easily into the countryside as if they were cottages. The railway became part of the landscape, its viaducts and bridges themselves were sights to see and admire. Railway-built structures stood, granite-firm, ready to last a thousand years. But there was one spectacular exception.

On the evening of Sunday 28th December 1879 a ferocious gale roared up the Firth of Tay in Scotland. Tiles were ripped from the rooftops in nearby Dundee and whirled in the air like paper, chimneys crashed to the ground and bathing huts were hurled from the shore out into the waters of the inky black River Tay. Until only two years previously railway travellers had needed to transfer to ferry boat for the Tay crossing before resuming their journey by train on the other side. Now there was a fine new railway bridge, over 3 km across and by far the longest in the world. At a little after 7.00 pm the last train of that fateful day, the 5.20 pm from Burntisland to Dundee, ran out on to the wondrous bridge. It was pitch dark and the wind howled as it tore in from the east, slapping the sides of the five-coach train like a giant's fist hitting a toy. Inside, its 70 passengers took heart that their journey would soon be over. The bridge was still a novelty, a source of amazement to be enjoyed by spectators even on a night such as this. People snug in houses along the shore turned down their lamps and peered through the dripping windows, watching as the lights of the train twinkled like stars dancing in the sky. Suddenly the lights were gone. The watchers rubbed their eyes in disbelief but slowly the awful truth dawned upon them: the Tay Bridge was down!

The central section of the bridge was known as the high girders. There the tracks ran inside a steel girder box set high enough to carry them above the main shipping lanes of the Tay. Empty, they were able to withstand the storm. As the train had passed through, however, wind pressure had increased on the larger area of solid material in its way. The gale had brought train and girders crashing into the water. Every single person aboard, passengers and staff, 75 men, women and children in all, perished in the cold black waters of the River Tay that fearful night.

The official Board of Trade inquiry into the accident placed the blame squarely on the shoulders of Sir Thomas Bouch, the bridge's designer. The Tay Bridge, it said, was 'badly designed, badly constructed and badly maintained'. Bouch was ruined. He had already built several viaducts that would last for nearly a century before needing dynamite to demolish them. Now he was removed from his greatest project, bridging the Firth of Forth. Soon afterwards he died, a broken man.

The engine that fell into the Tay was North British Railway No. 224. It was a fine locomotive, one of the first pair built to the inside-cylinder 4-4-0 design which would soon become the classic British type of the late Victorian era. Amazingly No. 224 was not a write-off and later it was recovered from its watery grave at the bottom of the Tay. Twice the chains dragging it to the surface

(*Above*) 'The Diver', North British Railway 4–4–0 No. 224. Built in 1871, it survived its ducking in the River Tay and ran until 1919.

(*Below*) The day after the Tay Bridge Disaster and the fruitless search continues for survivors. In the background is the gap where once the High Girders stood. 29 bodies were never recovered from the depths of the River Tay.

(*Above*) Locomotives with a single pair of huge driving wheels could reach high speeds with light trains. Most famous of all were the 'Stirling Singles' built for the Great Northern Railway by Patrick Stirling from 1870.

(*Below*) The Highland Railway was Britain's most northerly major line. This graceful 4–4–0 No. 71 *Clachnacuddin* was built in 1883 for service on the steeply-graded Perth to Inverness route.

snapped and it slid back below the waves as if reluctant to leave its new home on the sea bed. Eventually the battered locomotive was beached on the shore and children played about its rusting bulk. At last No. 224 was repaired and ran for another 40 years. With a fine sense of black humour crews nicknamed it 'the diver'. The high girders too were recovered. Some were used in the replacement bridge, others melted down and the metal used in the manufacture of locomotives, each of which bore a little commemorative plaque recording this curious fact.

The fall of the Tay Bridge was the only exception to the rule that Victorian railways were built to last. Within eight years there was another bridge spanning the Tay. It stands today, 3,552 m (2 miles 364 yds) in length, and the longest bridge on British Rail. As you travel over it look out of the train window and, just to the east, you will see the stumps of the first, ill-fated, Tay Bridge poking above the water.

Railways continued to change the lives of the British people. Bank holidays at last gave the working classes a first glimpse of leisure

time. As the Empire prospered there rose up a new relatively well-off, middle class with time and money to spare. Railways offered both social groups the opportunity to travel in their free moments. Coastal villages, for so long virtually cut-off from the rest of the country, flowered into seaside resorts as the trains brought holidaymakers and day trippers in their thousands. Tourism was a Victorian invention and a by-product of the coming of the railways.

Football league would not have been possible without trains to take its players and their supporters to away matches. Travel for business purposes increased and fast trains were scheduled for appropriate times. As the number of lines into the big cities increased, people moved away from their place of work. Suburbs grew up in what had previously been green fields. London marched out into the countryside and each day its people swarmed back into the centre. The railways made such residential travel financially attractive. There were cheap 'early morning' tickets for workmen and season tickets for the office staff. The commuter had been invented.

(*Above*) Great Western Railway 4–2–2 No. 3050 *Royal Sovereign* roars out of Box tunnel with an express in about 1910. Built in 1895, this fine locomotive ran for twenty years.

(*Below*) London & North Western Railway 2–2–2–2 No. 2053 *Greater Britain* was painted in post office red to work Queen Victoria's Diamond Jubilee train between Euston and Crewe in 1897. These engines had uncoupled driving wheels, each pair being driven independently.

(*Above*) Water troughs were laid between the rails at certain places so engines could pick up water without stopping, by using a special scoop in the tender. The leading engine of this double headed LNWR express is taking water as it overhauls a goods train.

(*Below*) A push and pull train of the Midland Railway. The driver's controls were in a compartment at the far end of each carriage and linked to the locomotive. The fireman remained on the engine.

Railways carried everything, indeed by law they had to accept any cargo offered to them. Britain was mother to an Empire 'on which the sun never set' and a giant factory for the world. Raw materials, coal, iron ore, finished goods, cattle, fish, beer, fruit and vegetables, meat, milk, mail and newspapers all went by train. It was cheap, easy and convenient. Without the railways to aid industry the country would never have grown as powerful as it did. The conveyance of coal was significant. The early waggonways had been devised to take coal from the pits only as far as the nearest river where it was transferred to ships. Now the railway, grown-up child of the waggonway, carried the coal all the way. From the ever-increasing numbers of mines of South Wales, the North East, Yorkshire and Scotland the coal trains rumbled by. Houses were warmed by coal fires, locomotives used coal, and it fuelled the furnaces of industry. The warships of the Grand Fleet used thousands of tons of these 'black diamonds' every time they set to sea.

The half-century from 1860 to 1910 saw great strides in locomotive development. A typical engine of the 1860s and 1870s had

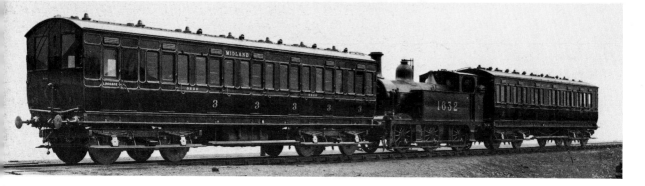

(*Left*) Euston station on the City and South London Railway, Britain's first deep-level 'tube', in 1908. It is now part of London Regional Transport's Northern Line.

four-coupled driving wheels and a leading pair under the smokebox. This 2-4-0 type was sufficient to haul the light trains of the day, but as bigger, heavier carriages were built more power was needed. By the 1880s there was the 4-4-0 type with its leading wheels mounted together on a truck, called a bogie, for greater stability. Larger boilers and wider fireboxes gave more power and the 4-4-0 became the classic express engine of the period. Gradually some form of protection was given to the crew, but the size of the cab varied considerably from railway to railway.

All the early locomotives had been fired with coke, but from the 1860s onwards coal took its place. The London & South Western Railway was one of the first to use this messy fuel and quickly earned the nickname 'blaze and smoke'. Beattie, the LSWR designer, used all sorts of complicated devices to aid combustion until it was real-

(*Above*) The Mersey Railway was opened in 1886 and on 3rd May 1903 became the first steam-worked underground railway to go over to electric traction. Today the line is part of the Merseyrail system.

(*Right*) Holyhead station, LNWR, where boat trains connected with ferries for Ireland, 1908. The six-wheeled coaches and privately-owned coal wagons were typical of this period. The building in the background is the LNWR's hotel.

(*Left*) Locomotives group round the turntable inside No. 4 roundhouse at Derby depot in 1909. Above them are massive ventilating shafts.

(*Above*) The driver's controls of Midland Railway 2–4–0 No. 10, built in 1876. Its cramped layout is typical of engines of the time.

ized that Matthew Kirtley on the Midland had already solved the problem. The knack of burning coal efficiently was to build a simple brick arch and firehole deflector plate into the firebox. Steel began to replace wrought iron in locomotive construction at this time too.

Soon after the turn of the century the Great Western Railway began to forge ahead, building locomotives with six-coupled driving wheels and outside cylinders — the 4-6-0 type. In 1908 they built Britain's first 4-6-2, or Pacific, type. This engine, No. 111 *The Great Bear* (named after the stars rather than the animal), was not popular and the GWR never built any more. It was another 20 years before the Pacific was established as *the* express passenger locomotive on most lines. There were many other wheel arrangements for different duties: 0-6-0 for shunting and goods, 2-8-0 for heavy freight and 0-4-4 tank engines for branch line or suburban trains, for example.

Engines needed places to be housed and locomotive depots or sheds of various sizes were built at strategic locations. Here engines were cleaned and took on coal and water between duties, or were stored when out of use. Simple repairs could be done at most larger depots. Engine crews and shed staff often lived in railway-owned houses nearby, and small boys were employed to call the men in time to start an early shift (a 3.00 am start was common). The earliest depots were of the circular roundhouse type with the tracks clustered around a turntable. Later long, straight buildings became more common. Train drivers started their careers as engine cleaners and gradually worked their way up to firemen; first on local and then on express services. On promotion to driver they reverted to unglamorous goods and slow passenger work before finally reaching the top job of express train driver.

Passenger comfort improved but it was a slow and patchy process. The ordinary carriage of the 1870s had no corridors, no lavatories,

(*Above*) A berth in a first class MR sleeping car of 1907. Third class sleeping cars were not introduced until 1928.

(*Left*) The interior of a first-class carriage used on the Euston to Glasgow expresses.

(*Above*) Up for the cup.

no fixed heating (you might get a foot-warmer, a kind of metal hot water bottle) and illumination only from unsavoury oil-pot lamps. The difference between first and third class was still much the same as twenty years before. Better things were on the way for the first class passenger. Luxurious Pullman parlour cars, imported from America, were introduced on trains between London St Pancras and Bradford on 1st June 1874. They contained easy chairs and lavatories, and could provide meals if these were ordered in advance. Five years later the first real dining car was put into service in Britain. Called *Prince of Wales*, this Pullman car possessed a fully equipped kitchen and commenced running from London King's Cross to Leeds, Great Northern Railway, on 1st November 1879.

Usually only one or two Pullmans were included in the crack expresses. The exception was on the London, Brighton & South Coast Railway where a train made up entirely of Pullman cars was introduced in December 1881. It was also the first train in this country to be electrically-lit throughout. Its use of electric light was exceptional though. From the 1880s oil-gas lighting, similar to that used in homes, was adopted for carriages. It would be seventy years before the last gas-lit vehicles finally disappeared. After 1890 a form

(*Above*) Each railway company had its own coat of arms and used it on everything from locomotives to chamber pots!
(*Below*) GWR elegance: *Knight of the Golden Fleece*.

A stern warning from the Cheshire Lines Committee.

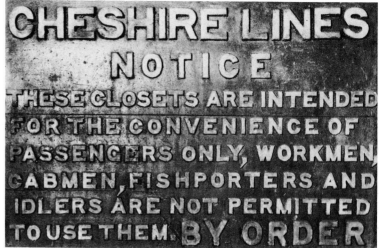

(*Above*) The GWR ran the first railway-operated buses in 1903 and were soon followed by other companies.

(*Above*) Guards of the Midland Railway about 1910.

of heating using steam from the locomotive piped through the train was gradually introduced. Corridors began to appear within coaches to give access to a centrally placed lavatory. Side corridor coaches followed and on 7th March 1892 the Great Western Railway ran the first all-corridor train with connecting gangways throughout. A sleeping car for first class passengers only was put in service in 1873. The interior resembled a Victorian bedroom complete with huge brass bedstead. As the carriages grew larger and heavier they needed more wheels to support them. Wheels were grouped in bogies and set at either end to give a more comfortable ride.

By the Edwardian era railway carriages varied wildly from the very good to the decidedly awful. A few railways, the Midland in particular, provided excellent accommodation for their third class passengers. In general, however, third class carriages were rare on express trains.

Continuous brakes, which came on automatically if the carriages broke apart, were developed slowly. A disastrous accident at Armagh in 1889 caused by inadequate brakes eventually spurred the government into compelling all railways to adopt continuous brakes. There were other new safety measures. As the number of tracks and trains increased, signalmen were removed from the trackside and stationed in control boxes. In these signalboxes they controlled levers connected by rods and wires to the signals which were some distance away. Points, a section of track which switches trains from one line to another, were interlocked with the signals that guarded them. At bigger stations or junctions where there were too many signals to be placed beside the tracks without confusion they were mounted on steel girders, called gantries, set above the lines.

Steel rails began to take over from iron, their first experimental use was at Derby on the Midland Railway in 1857. By 1910 typical main line track was formed of steel rails in short lengths of around 20 m (60 feet) bolted together by small iron sections called fishplates.

(*Left*) The staff at Water Orton station pose for the camera in about 1903. Even a relatively small station could boast a large staff at this time. Note the railway policeman.

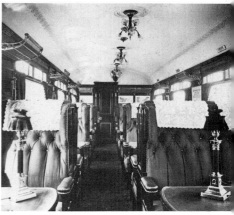

(*Above*) Interior of North Eastern Railway dining car No. 1140 built in 1909.

The rails rested on cast-iron supports or chairs which were secured to wooden planks or sleepers. The complete track was set in a bed of granite chips known as ballast.

Although the railways of Britain were almost 100 per cent steam operated, by 1914 electricity had begun to make its mark as an alternative. Britain's first all-electric railway was opened by Magnus Volk at Brighton on 4th August 1883. It ran for only a short distance along the seafront, but gave a convincing demonstration of the potential of electric traction. The advantages of the electric railway — clean and pollution-free — were recognized immediately by the builders of London's first 'deep level' tube. This was the City & South London Railway whose first section, between King William Street and Stockwell, opened on 4th November 1890. It was a great

(*Below*) The most remote line in Britain was possibly the 68.6 cm (2′ 3″) gauge Campbeltown & Machrihanish Light Railway on the Mull of Kintyre in Scotland. Built originally to carry coal, it later had a heavy traffic in tourists but eventually closed in 1932.

(*Left*) Great Eastern Railway locomotives were painted in a beautiful shade of blue even down to this little 0–6–0T built for working suburban trains out of Liverpool St.

success and compared favourably with the smoke-ridden Metropolitan Railway. The 'Met', which had commenced operations on 10th January 1863, was labelled the world's first underground line, but in reality was only in a deep cutting partly covered over. Even so the use of steam locomotives in such a confined area kept its platforms in a perpetual fog.

The first British suburban electrification was between Newcastle and Benton, North Eastern Railway, opened on 29th March 1904. Close behind came the Lancashire & Yorkshire Railway's Liverpool to Southport line on 5th April. The London, Brighton & South Coast Railway started services on a 6,600 volt ac overhead system

(*Above*) Many of the Lancashire & Yorkshire Railway's heavy expresses were worked by 2–4–2 tank engines. This is the first of them, No. 1008, dating from 1889 and now preserved.

(*Below*) Great Central Railway 4–4–0 No. 506 *Butler-Henderson.*

between Victoria and London Bridge (the South London line) on 1st December 1909. Carriages with motors fitted inside drew electricity via an arm called a pantograph from conductor wires set on overhead gantries similar to those used for signals. Six years later, on 23rd October 1915, its neighbour the London & South Western Railway commenced running on a 600 volt dc system, picking up power from a third rail set beside the tracks. It was not until the railway amalgamation of 1923 that some standardization of equipment on the south London lines was achieved.

The railway companies' interests spread far beyond trains alone.

(*Above*) North Eastern Railway 4–4–0 No. 1621 took part in the Railway Race to the North in 1895. Like all the locomotives shown on these two pages it is now preserved. (*Below*) In all the splendour of the Midland Railway 'crimson lake' livery, 4–4–0 compound No. 1000, built in 1914.

(*Right*) The solidly-built station at Machynlleth on the Cambrian Railway in mid-Wales, July 1909.

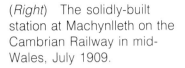

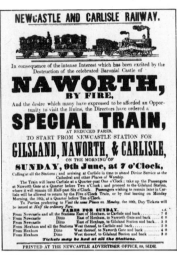

(*Above*) Off to see the ruins. A poster advertising an excursion to see the remains of Naworth Castle, recently destroyed by fire in 1844.

(*Above*) All dressed up and nowhere to go. LT & SR 4–4–2T No. 80 *Thundersley*, adorned for the Coronation of King George V, at Upminster in June 1911.

As railways in Britain and France reached the coast, cross-channel ferry services were introduced to connect the two systems. The very first railway ships were those of the Chester & Holyhead Railway. They started sailing between Holyhead and Kingstown (now Dun Laoghaire) on 1st January 1848 and offered a through service to Ireland connecting with the 'Irish Mail' express from Euston. Docks such as Dover and Southampton expanded dramatically in size as the railways increased the scale of their operations.

The first railway hotel was opened at Euston in 1841, and by 1900 most of the major companies owned fine establishments in the big cities, usually next to the station. Stations, especially the larger ones, became more enjoyable places to linger in. The first bookstall was set up by W H Smith in 1848. Refreshment rooms, originally let to outside caterers but later owned by the railways themselves, were soon to be found almost everywhere. They can trace their origins back to the inns situated at intervals along the old stage-coach routes. Before the use of dining cars became widespread the most important trains would stop for about 20 minutes at York or Preston so passengers could rush into the refreshment room and gobble down a meal.

But the glamour of those far-off days lay with the trains themselves and in particular their elegant, peacock-coloured locomotives. The spur for them to achieve great things was provided by the cut-throat competition between certain rival companies. Let us re-enter our time machine and go back to Carlisle Citadel station. It is a little longer ago than on our first visit; just turned half-past midnight on 23rd August 1895 and at the climax of the Railway Race to the North.

For six weeks the East and West Coast routes have been battling it out for the money-spinning overnight traffic to Aberdeen. Each evening, trains have left Euston and King's Cross at 8.00 pm to roar through the night until finally one passes the winning post at

Kinnaber Junction, a lonely signalbox where the two routes converge just 61 km (38 miles) from Aberdeen. Timetables have been thrown out of the window. The trains stop at intermediate stations only long enough to change engines or take water. Unwary passengers who stray too far are liable to return and find their train already racing away into the darkness. On every night, bar one, the West Coast partners, the London & North Western and the Caledonian railways, have put up the better performance. Last night was the exception when the East Coast companies (Great Northern, North Eastern and North British railways) beat them by a full fifteen minutes into Aberdeen. The East Coast group have immediately

(*Above*) A London, Brighton & South Coast Railway electric train at Victoria. The second vehicle is the power car. Most of the adverts festooning the walls are made of enamel.

(*Left*) An early view of the first electric railway in Britain, opened by Magnus Volk in 1883. It still runs along the seafront at Brighton and has never been part of the main railway network.

Preserved locomotives capture the splendour and colour that marked the pre-grouping era.

(*Left*) Midland Railway 4–2–2 No. 673, built in 1899. These engines were known as 'Spinners' because of the graceful way their large driving wheels revolved at speed.

(*Right*) The first British locomotives of the 4–4–2, or Atlantic wheel arrangement, were built by the Great Northern Railway in 1898. Four years later came No. 251, the first of a more powerful type which ran for nearly 50 years. No. 251 was eventually preserved but returned briefly to the tracks in 1954 and is seen here at Edge Hill.

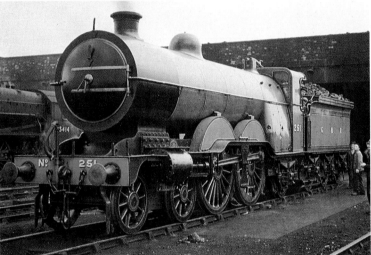

(*Left*) High in the Pennines, Ribblehead station once served as a weather reporting centre for the Air Ministry. Typical of many wayside stations with buildings on one platform only, it changed little during its long existence. This photograph was taken in 1967.

Between 1958 and 1965 the Scottish Region of British Railways ran regular excursions with four fully-restored veteran engines. They are all now in the Glasgow Museum of Transport.

(*Right*) Highland Railway No. 103 was the first 4–6–0 engine to run in Britain. Designed in 1894 by David Jones for goods traffic it was always known as the 'Jones Goods'. Here it is at Kinloss in 1962.

(*Left*) Caledonian Railway 4–2–2 No. 123 was built in 1886 and took part in the first Race to Scotland two years later. For many years it was the royal pilot engine running ahead of the royal train to ensure the tracks were clear. The 'Caley Single' ran until 1935 and was the first Scottish veteran to return to the tracks. Two CR coaches were restored to go with it and one can be seen in this 1962 picture.

(*Right*) North British Railway 4–4–0 No. 256 *Glen Douglas* was built in 1913 and is seen working a special train for railway enthusiasts at Dunfermline Lower station in 1963. For many years these elegant locomotives ran on the West Highland Line.

(*Above*) A Midland Railway express of 1880. The second vehicle is a Pullman Drawing Car introduced six years earlier.

North Eastern Railway locomotives of the mid-Victorian era:

(*Above*) 4–4–0 No. 376 built in 1884, at York.

(*Right*) 0–6–0 No. 1275, built in 1874. These 'long-boiler' goods engines were known as the 'Hippopotamus' class.

shouted truce but no one at Euston in listening. That single defeat must be avenged.

Now, as the Carlisle station clock ticks off the minutes, ears are strained for the sound of the West Coast flyer. It left Euston dead on time behind LNWR compound 2-2-2-0 No. 1309 *Adriatic* and headed out into the teeth of a thunderstorm. At Crewe, engines were changed and the tiny 2-4-0 No. 790 *Hardwicke* blazed into the darkness, topping the formidable climb to Shap summit at over 65 kph (40 mph) and hitting 129 kph (80 mph) downhill.

Suddenly the gleaming black locomotive is in, screeching to a halt as young Fireman Wolstencroft leaps down to uncouple. Driver 'Big Ben' Robinson has averaged 108.6 kph (67½ mph) start-to-stop over the difficult 227 km (141 miles) from Crewe.

Within two and a half minutes Driver Archibald 'Baldie' Crooks is opening the regulator on Caledonian Railway 4-4-0 No. 90 and storming away to do battle with the steep gradients of Beattock Bank. At Perth he will hand over to sixty-year-old John Soutar on 4-4-0 No. 17 who then races the final leg into Aberdeen. On arrival in the Granite City at 4.32 am the white-bearded Soutar will be carried shoulder high by the cheering crowd. The whole journey from Euston to Aberdeen has been covered in an amazing 512 minutes for the 869 km (540 miles). It is a record average speed of 101.8 kph (63.3 mph) over the vast distance that will remain unbroken throughout the steam era.

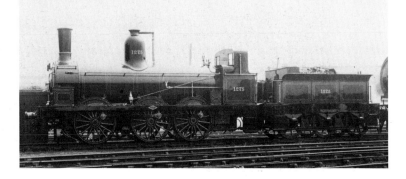

(*Left*) The first engines to burn oil were on the Great Eastern Railway in 1898. It was an economical way of disposing of the waste from the oil-gas lighting.

Eight years after the drama of the Race to the North, rivalry between two other railways was responsible for a further piece of record-breaking. In those pre-jumbo-jet days the only way to travel from America to Europe was by one of the giant, four-funnelled transatlantic steamers. Around 1903 certain of the German steamships began to make Plymouth their first British port of call. Here urgent mails were taken off and passengers in a hurry could leave the ship also and dash up to London by special train.

The Great Western Railway and the London & South Western Railway each had a route to the capital, and competition for this American traffic was bitter. Eventually they reached a gentlemen's agreement that the GWR would take the mails and the LSWR would carry the passengers. It was a matter of fierce pride however who got their precious cargo to London first. During April 1904 the LSWR had put up a particularly fast run, beating all the GWR's previous efforts. Soon the GWR were out for revenge, and they didn't have to look far for an excuse. Steaming majestically into

(*Above*) Smallest of the seven railways to use Carlisle Citadel station in pre-grouping days, was the Maryport & Carlisle. This is their 0–4–2 No. 5 built in 1873.

(*Below*) The GWR built large numbers of tank engines of the 2–6–2 or Prairie type for its suburban services. This is No. 3141, one of the first, dating from 1907.

(*Above*) Saddle tanks were so called because the tank was placed astride the boiler like a saddle on a horse's back. *Bismarck*, was used in the construction of new lines.

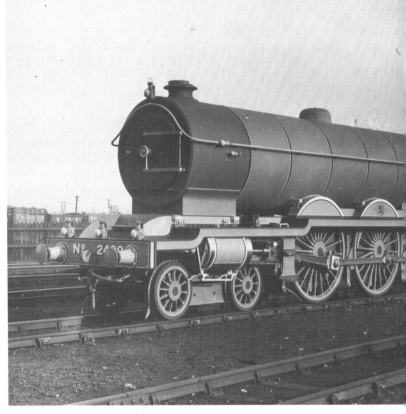

(*Above*) LNWR No. 790 *Hardwicke*, hero of the 1895 Race to the North, is preserved in working order.

(*Right*) On 1st July 1915 the North Eastern Railway electrified its coal-carrying Shildon to Newport (Teesside) line. It also had grand plans to electrify the York–Darlington main line but these came to nothing. The Shildon electrification was eventually abandoned in 1935 when the freight traffic disappeared during the economic slump.

Plymouth Sound came the mighty *Kronprinz Wilhelm* of the crack North German Lloyd Line. Part of her cargo was gold; a massive shipment of bullion from America to France as payment for the recently-purchased Panama Canal. Needed in London, that gold provided the ideal reason for a record-breaking run. So at 9.23 pm on the night of 9th May 1904 Driver Clements opened the regulator on his 4-4-0 No. 3440 *City of Truro* and proceeded to race into the pages of history. Charles Rous-Marten, a freelance locomotive expert, travelled on the train using stopwatches to note speeds and times.

The initial stretch, over the switchback of steep climbs and vicious curves of South Devon, was run in record time. Then beyond Exeter things really hotted up and the little engine took the long climb to Whiteball Summit at full tilt. Once over the top Clements let her rip. On the easy grades descending Wellington Bank she tore along, speeds mounting by the second. Rous-Marten's excitement rose to fever-pitch then his stopwatches recorded the magic figure of 164.6 kph (102.3 mph). At that very moment *City of Truro's* whistle went berserk and the brakes were slammed on as Clements sighted a group of workmen on the tracks in the distance. What the maximum might have been but for this check remains a matter for argument even today.

Also a subject for heated discussion is whether Rous-Marten got it quite right. Did *City of Truro* hit exactly 102.3 mph? No amount of scientific analysis, however, can dispute that for the first time a British train had breached the 100 mph barrier. *City of Truro* was our first ton-up train. The steam railway was all powerful but its days were numbered.

(*Above*) In 1922 Sir Vincent Raven designed a type of powerful new 'Pacific' for the North Eastern Railway. The first, No. 2400, appeared just before the grouping when the NER became part of the LNER. New locomotive chief of the LNER was Nigel Gresley who had his own ideas about 'Pacifics', and Raven's engines did not last long. This is No. 2400, brand new, before receiving its name *City of Newcastle*.

(*Right*) Birthplace of No. 2400 and many fine engines for over a century was Darlington Works, seen here in NER days – about 1910.

5 Paradise lost

On 28th July 1914, at Sarajevo in what is now Yugoslavia, a young student named Gavrilo Princip fired two shots that were eventually to result in the deaths of ten million men, women and children. The immediate targets for his bullets were the Archduke Franz Ferdinand, heir to the throne of Austria, and his wife. Both died at once on a sunny afternoon that marked not only their fourteenth wedding anniversary but also the start of the First World War.

War between the Great Powers of Europe had been brewing for years and this excuse to begin hostilities was eagerly seized. A few days later Germany invaded Belgium on its march towards France;

Preparing for an invasion that never came: this armoured train was built by the LNWR at Crewe in 1914.

Britain, sworn by treaty to protect Belgian neutrality, declared war on Germany on 4th August. It was a bank holiday weekend and in Britain the trains were crowded with holidaymakers heading for the seaside and the sun. Few people could have told you where Sarajevo was; none realized that four years of hell lay ahead and nothing, not least the railways, would ever be quite the same again.

Plans for the control of Britain's independent railways in the event of war had been laid well in advance. A Railway Executive Committee made up of the general managers of ten major lines would be in overall charge and responsible to the government. As

(*Above*) Lady ticket collectors at Waterloo in 1915.

(*Below*) A train of the Bideford, Westward Ho! & Appledore Railway in Devon. This line closed in 1917 and its rails were lifted and sent to the Western Front for use by the military railways.

the strokes of midnight sounded the last seconds of peace that night, the REC took over the running of 130 railway companies. Their empire ranged from the mighty North Eastern to the tiny Freshwater, Yarmouth & Newport Railway on the Isle of Wight.

In 1914 the railways of the United Kingdom possessed a total of 22,998 locomotives which represented one for almost every route mile. Rolling stock consisted of 72,888 carriages and 1.4 million goods wagons. By today's standards it was a lavishly equipped system, but in war such over-provision of resources is an advantage. Things began with a rush. Thousands of members of the territorial army were away at camp in remote parts of the country that weekend. Some had scarcely arrived before they were heading back to base again to await transport to the war zone. By the end of August 118,000 troops of the British Expeditionary Force and their equipment had been conveyed in 670 special trains to Southampton where they embarked for France.

After this initial flurry of activity it was business as usual for a while. During the 1914–18 war the mainland of Britain and its civilians never suffered as they did in the second great conflict. There were air raids, first by Zeppelins and later by aeroplanes, but although damage was widespread it was also light. Twenty-four railwaymen were killed on duty during bombing raids but at no time was the system brought to a halt. More of a problem were the thousands of staff who rushed to enlist in the armed forces at the outbreak of war. By 1915 the railways were being pressed to release extra men, and later conscription took even more. The gap was filled by women. In 1914 there were just over 13,000 at work on Britain's railways, mostly employed in the hotels and restaurants or as secretaries. Now, with the men away fighting, women were taken on to clean engines and carriages or act as porters. At the end of the war over 68,000 were employed, but they gave up their places when men returned home.

Over 184,000 railwaymen joined the forces, almost one third of the total staff, and of that number 21,522 died for their country.

(*Left*)   One of the London &
South Western Railway's
carriage cleaners smiles at the
camera from the doorway of
a typical wooden-bodied
coach in 1915. Points to note
are the leather strap for raising
or lowering the window, the
'smoking' sign and the
massive footboard which ran
the whole length of the
carriage

(*Above*)   The memorial at
Liverpool Street station to
Captain Fryatt who was shot
by the Germans in 1916.

After the war, memorials to the dead were placed on many major
stations. Several companies also dedicated a locomotive to the fallen.

Some 40,000 of the railwaymen who joined up continued to do
railway work abroad. Railways were a vital method of moving men
and machinery from supply bases to as near the fighting as possible.
New lines were built, others upgraded or repaired. The Railway
Operating Division was formed to co-ordinate and run this network
of railway lines behind the front lines. During the second half of
the war there was a shortage of French and Belgian motive power
and locomotives were sent out from Britain. A total of 601 engines
eventually went abroad. Not all were sent to the Western Front
(France and Belgium), some also went to the Middle East. Most
were rather elderly 0-6-0 freight engines, but the Great Western
Railway managed to spare some new 2-6-0s, one of which is now
preserved at the Didcot Railway Centre. The ROD also ordered a
large number of 2-8-0 heavy freight engines identical to the Great

(*Above*) Streatham Common signalbox on 14th September 1916 after being damaged by a bomb. Air-raids were few during the First World War compared to 1939–1945, but no less destructive.

Central Railway Class 8K. They were built by private firms; only 311 actually went to war, the remaining 210 being delivered after hostilities ended.

Most of the engines that served on the Western Front were eventually returned to this country. Brand new 2-8-0s were dumped in sidings all over Britain, items in a giant war surplus sale. Most were bought by the Great Central; the London & North Western and the Great Western each had some, a few went to China, and 19 even went to Australia where they ran, virtually unaltered, until recently. The North British Railway had the happy idea of giving their returning 0-6-0 goods engines names associated with the war. There were *Ypres* and *Verdun*, named after battles; *Ole Bill*, a famous soldier cartoon character; and one called *Maude*. This was no lady but the surname of a general. Built in 1891, she lasted until the end of steam and is now preserved in full working order. In 1984 she hauled special trains on the West Highland line in Scotland.

Locomotive names also reflected the anti-German hysteria that characterized civilian response to the war. The LNWR engine *Germanic* was renamed *Belgic*. To hammer home the point the original nameplate was retained with a red line painted through it and the *Belgic* plate fixed above. The same fate befell their *Dachshund*, which changed breeds to become a thoroughly British *Bulldog*.

The South Eastern & Chatham Railway kept quiet about its latest batch of Class L 4-4-0s, which had been built by Borsig of Berlin and delivered just before the outbreak of war.

Hundreds of thousands of fighting men were carried safely by train during the war years. In view of this fine record it is all the more tragic that the only serious mishap involving a troop train should also have been the worst ever accident on a British railway. It occurred on 22nd May 1915 at Quintinshill, a remote signalbox just over the border in Scotland, not far from Gretna Green. An early morning local train from Carlisle had to be shunted there out of the way of the late-running Euston to Glasgow overnight express which was close behind. In normal circumstances the local would have been put in one of the two loop lines but both were already occupied by freight trains. The signalman quite correctly switched the local to the up line so it was facing north on the southbound track. Inexplicably he then forgot it was there and cleared the signals for a southbound troop train. This contained 485 soldiers, half a battalion, of the Royal Scots regiment who were travelling to Liverpool where they were to board ship for Gallipoli and the invasion of Turkey.

Running downhill at high speed the troop train rounded the sweeping curve just north of Quintinshill and hit the local head on. The terrific impact reduced the train to matchwood and debris was strewn across both tracks. Worse was to follow. A minute later, even as a few dazed soldiers began to struggle desperately out of the mangled carriages, the northbound express which was double-headed ran into the wreckage. The second collision was as frightful as the first; gas leaked from the smashed carriages and was set alight by hot coals spilled from the locomotives. The fire raged for over

(*Above*)　Quintinshill, near Gretna, 22nd May 1915. Coaches smoulder in the aftermath of Britain's worst ever railway accident.

(*Below*)　War Surplus R.O.D. 2–8–0 No. 1733 (based on the Great Central Railway's heavy freight engines) finds temporary employment on the London & South Western Railway at Strawberry Hill depot in July 1920. The LSWR had several on loan after the war but did not buy any.

(*Above*) Several companies dedicated a locomotive to staff who had been killed in the war. On the LNWR it was named *Patriot*, the Great Central engine was *Valour* and that of the LB & SCR was called *Remembrance*. This is *Valour* photographed at Neasden in August 1937, some years after the Great Central had been absorbed into the LNER.

24 hours and consumed not only most of the three passenger trains but many of the adjacent goods wagons as well. In all 227 people died, 215 of them soldiers from the troop train. It was a disaster for the Royal Scots and it can have been of little comfort to the bereaved that the men were killed on their way to near certain death. For the other half of the battalion suffered almost total losses when it arrived at Gallipoli.

Railway shipping was badly disrupted during the war. Many vessels were requisitioned by the Admiralty and put to use carrying troops and supplies or acting as ambulance ships. Others were converted into mine-layers or mine-sweepers and three little Humber ferries even became seaplane carriers.

On 23rd June 1916 the Germans captured the Great Eastern Railway steamship *Brussels* and put her master, Captain C A Fryatt, on trial. He was accused of ramming and sinking a submarine the previous year, an act of sabotage as he was a civilian. After a speedy and biased hearing he was sentenced to death on 27th July and shot that same evening. Once the war was over his body was brought home and is now buried at Dovercourt. A plaque in his memory is on display at Liverpool Street station.

During the second half of the war the absence of so many staff began to make itself felt. There were widespread cuts in services and schedules were slowed down considerably. Many restaurant and sleeping cars were taken off altogether. A few little-used suburban stations had been closed in 1914–15, but now some minor lines were shut down. There was a demand for rail at the front and surplus tracks were lifted.

Although the REC published notices requesting the public not to travel unnecessarily during the war there was never the propaganda campaign of 1939–45.

A minor record established during the war was the running of the longest ever through trains yet seen in Britain. These were specials from Euston to Thurso, 1,154 km (717 miles), conveying sailors to the great naval base at nearby Scapa Flow. All ships were coal-fired at that time and there was also a never-ending procession of coal trains labouring up the steeply graded Highland Railway main line north of Perth.

Building of new locomotives continued throughout the war, although most workshops were also producing shells and other war materials. After the war ended, positions were reversed and a batch of engines was constructed at the great Woolwich Arsenal in an effort to ease the run-down of work there.

The war ended on 11th November 1918 with the Armistice (a cease-fire) and peace was declared on 23rd June 1919. Only two years later services and schedules on nearly all lines had been restored to what they had been in 1914. But things would never be the same again. Working Britain's many railways under the single control of the REC had shown how wasteful the old methods of cut-throat competition had been. And there were new rivals to contend with. Heavy lorries had improved dramatically in the last four years and many were now being bought as army surplus by ex-soldiers intent on starting their own haulage businesses. There was even talk of a London to Paris air service using ex-RAF bombers.

Nationalization of the railways was discussed but rejected. It was just after the Russian revolution and any form of socialism smacked of Bolshevism and was not to be tolerated. So there was a compromise, and on 19th August 1921 an Act of Parliament was passed declaring that over 120 companies should merge into just four. The date for this grouping of Britain's railways was set for 1st January 1923.

(*Below*) North British Railways 0–6–0 No. 673 *Maude*, named after a First World War general, is preserved in full working order. Here it steams through Locheilside with a West Highland line special in July 1984.

6 The Big Four

Four great railways were created by the grouping of 1st January 1923. They were the Great Western Railway (GWR), the Southern Railway (SR), the London, Midland & Scottish Railway (LMSR) and the London & North Eastern Railway (LNER). Between them they absorbed 123 different, often very individualistic companies. Lines which had traditionally been bitter rivals now found themselves merged. The old names disappeared, locomotives and rolling stock lost the liveries they had carried for so long in favour of new colour schemes. It was a time of drastic readjustment.

Pride of the LMSR, 4–6–0 No. 6113 *Cameronian* climbs Beattock Bank with the non-stop Euston to Glasgow run of the 'Royal Scot' on 28th April 1928.

(*Above*)   A number of British locomotives have toured America. Here the 'Broadway Limited' escorts the 'Royal Scot' out of Harrisburg on 19th May 1933.

(*Above*)   Largest class on the GWR were the 0–6–0 pannier tanks of which 863 were built. No. 9769 heads down the main line with a lengthy mixed freight in the 1930s.

The Big Four, as the new railway companies were known to public and railway staff alike, existed for exactly 25 years. In that quarter-century they faced many difficulties, including the years of industrial depression, the Second World War and ever-increasing competition from road transport. It was also a very exciting time. There was much modernization of locomotives, coaches, signalling, track and stations. The jewels in the crown so far as passenger services are concerned were the high-speed expresses described in the next chapter. Within a few years the Big Four railways had each created so strong an identity that no railway-minded person could fail to distinguish one from another. And although from Wick to Penzance steam reigned very nearly supreme, other forms of motive power were slowly being developed that would lead eventually to the all-diesel and electric railway of today.

Biggest of the Big Four was the LMSR. It was made up of the former London & North Western, Midland, Caledonian, Glasgow & South Western, and Highland railways. There were also smaller local lines including the North Staffordshire and Furness railways. The whole of the Anglo-Scottish West Coast route now belonged to the LMSR, whose trains also served Manchester, Liverpool, Birmingham, Nottingham, North Wales, Oban, Inverness and the far north of Scotland. They also inherited a couple of railways in Ireland. 'Crimson lake' (a deep shade of red) was chosen as the new colour for the LMSR's express passenger locomotives and carriages. This was the same livery as the old Midland Railway had used and it caused some ill-feeling among staff who had previously been with its deadly rival the London & North Western Railway. The feud between former staff of these two railways was the only serious

(*Left*) With over 400 locomotives allocated there, Stratford depot in East London was the largest on the LNER.

instance of old loyalties interfering with the smooth running of any of the new companies.

Second largest of the Big Four was the LNER, formed by amalgamating the Great Northern, Great Eastern, Great Central, North Eastern, North British and Great North of Scotland railways, together with several smaller lines. The LNER included the whole of the East Coast main line from King's Cross to Edinburgh. Its trains ran to Aberdeen, Elgin, Mallaig, the industrial North East of England, the East Midlands, Yorkshire and East Anglia. LNER express passenger engines were painted in the grass green livery of the old Great Northern Railway, but it didn't seem to upset anyone else. Main line carriages had the bodysides panelled in varnished teak to give a most distinctive appearance.

Third in size but playing second fiddle to no one in importance

(*Above*) Many odd-looking experimental engines were tried out in the 1920s and 1930s. This is the Beyer Peacock-Ljungström steam turbine during trials at St Pancras in 1927.
(*Below*) A new look in stations. Wimbledon Chase on the Southern Electric.

was the Great Western Railway. Alone among the Big Four it retained its old title after the grouping. For the GWR, grouping consisted of little more than an opportunity to take over various local Welsh lines. In fact it didn't wait until 1923 but swallowed up the Taff Vale, Cambrian, Rhymney and Cardiff railways, as well as some smaller fry, a whole year earlier.

As before, the GWR controlled main lines from London to Bristol, South Wales, Penzance, Worcester, Gloucester and Birmingham. It almost monopolized South and Mid Wales and much of the West Country. Not surprisingly its locomotives continued to be painted the same shade of Brunswick green with plenty of well-polished brasswork and copper caps to the chimneys. Coaching stock remained in the delicious-sounding colour combination of chocolate and cream.

Smallest and most compact of the Big Four was the Southern Railway. It brought together the London, Brighton & South Coast, London & South Western, and South Eastern & Chatham railways, as well as the three tiny companies which had operated independently on the Isle of Wight. The SR controlled the whole of Southern England from Kent to Hampshire, and its lines thrust into Dorset, Devon and Cornwall to rival the mighty GWR. Main line SR locomotives and coaches were also painted green but a different shade from those used by the LNER and GWR. The SR experimented with various greens, one of which was discontinued because it turned blue when exposed to the sea air for too long. As most SR routes ended at the coast their coaches tended to spend rather a lot of time in sidings close to the sea.

(*Above*)   Interior of a first class carriage built in 1928 for the LMSR 'Royal Scot' express.

(*Above*)   The coaling tower at Bushbury depot in 1941. Coal was discharged automatically into the locomotive beneath.

(*Left*) Steam railcars combined a locomotive unit and carriage body into one unit. A variety of types were built and used mainly on branch lines.

Bigger, more powerful steam locomotives were built throughout the years of the Big Four. On the GWR and LNER it was a smooth process of development from existing types. The GWR 'Castle' and 'King' classes looked every bit the classic express passenger 4-6-0 that had been emerging from Swindon Works since the turn of the century. Smaller versions, the 'Halls' and 'Granges', were built for secondary lines, and neat little tank engines could be seen on branch lines all over the system.

The LNER continued the 'big engine' policy established by its locomotive chief Nigel Gresley when he was in charge at the Great Northern Railway. Locomotives of the Pacific or 4-6-2 wheel arrangement, capable of sustained high-speed running and heavy

(*Below*) To avoid using two engines on its heaviest freight trains, the LMSR bought 33 engines of the Beyer Garratt type in 1927. Each engine had two sets of wheels with a water tank placed ahead of boiler. This is 2–6–0 + 0–6–2 No. 47996 pictured towards the end of its existence in the 1950s, by which time it was a British Railways engine.

(*Right*) Dawn of the diesels. A line-up of 0–6–0 diesel shunters at an LMSR marshalling yard in 1939. The LMSR pioneered this type of locomotive in 1931.

(*Above*) In 1934 the GWR introduced some streamlined diesel railcars. Here one poses at Paddington beside a mighty 'King' class 4–6–0 No. 6001 *King Edward VII*.

haulage, were built in large numbers. Later we will tell the story of their record-breaking efforts on crack expresses.

Both the LMSR and SR started at a disadvantage. The LMSR inherited a mixed bag of elderly and underpowered locomotives from both the LNWR and the Midland Railway. The Midland in particular had always built small engines and put two of them on nearly every fast train. The motive power crisis was averted by the introduction of the famous 'Royal Scot' class 4-6-0s built in 1927 to haul the top LMSR expresses including the Euston–Glasgow train of the same name. Larger Pacific types were designed in the 1930s, by which time the LMSR was well on its way to standardizing its locomotive fleet with new go-anywhere, do-anything engines to replace the veterans.

Facing much the same problem as the LMSR, the SR developed a 1918 London & South Western Railway 4-6-0 design into its 'King Arthur' class. These engines all bore the names of Knights of the Round Table or places associated with the Arthurian legend. The names were thought up by the SR's publicity department as a way of advertising the fact that their trains served North Cornwall where Arthur is supposed to have lived. Later SR types included the very

(*Below*) The experimental LMSR diesel train which underwent trials in 1938.

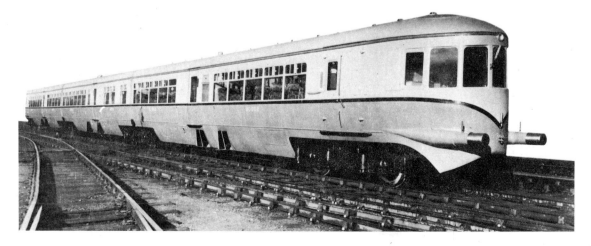

powerful 'Lord Nelson' class and the two streamlined Pacific classes
built during and just after the Second World War.

The Big Four companies continued building steam locomotives
because coal was cheap and plentiful. There were also large numbers
of staff available at depots to undertake the dirty and time-
consuming process of lighting-up a locomotive at the beginning of
its duties. Raking out its fire and emptying the smokebox of ash at
the end of the shift were also filthy and unpleasant jobs. The atmos-
phere inside a steam shed could resemble a smoky hell at times.

Electrification of suburban lines had already taken off on the
Southern Railway. The chalky soil south of the Thames is unsuitable
for building underground railways, so the SR had South London
and the area beyond to itself. They continued the policy begun by
the LSWR in 1915 of electrifying routes using a third-rail system
which was simpler and cheaper to instal than overhead wires.
'Southern Electric' soon became a brand name for excellence. Quiet,
clean, comfortable and fast, their electric multiple-units (the power
equipment was contained within certain of the coaches) spread out
beyond the inner city and into the suburbs, and the suburbs
followed the railway. Housing development went hand-in-hand with

The Big Four take on the
opposition.

(*Above*)   A Railway Air
Services plane at Speke
Aerodrome near Liverpool in
1941.

(*Below*)   A line-up of brand
new buses for use on LMSR
operated services in various
parts of the country, 1928.

(*Right*)   Channel Islands boat trains still run through the streets of Weymouth to Quay station where the ferries await. This was the scene in GWR days.

(*Left*)   Part of the LNER's large fleet of road vehicles.

(*Below*)   LNER 4–6–0 No. 10000 had an experimental boiler and was built in conditions of great secrecy in 1929. This lead to it being nicknamed the 'hush-hush' engine.

electrification; estate agents found it a major selling point to potential customers. At a time when there was rarely more than one car-owning family in each street, having a Southern Electric station nearby was a major temptation to buy.

The SR electrification plans did not stop at the suburbs. On 1st January 1933 they inaugurated services on Britain's first electrified inter-city line, between Victoria and Brighton. Out went steam, to be replaced by new electric trains including the all-Pullman 'Brighton Belle'. Four years later the SR electrified the Portsmouth line, but war put a stop to its other wide-ranging plans for more electrification.

Diesel-powered locomotives were tried out in a small way by all four railways. In 1931 the LMSR rebuilt a 'Jinty' steam locomotive into an 0-6-0 diesel shunter with mechanical transmission. The other railways followed suit, producing similar diesel shunters to a basic

(*Above*) LNER Class 'V2' 2–6–2 No. 4843 *Kings Own Yorkshire Light Infantry*. These excellent engines were designed by Nigel Gresley for use on both express passenger and freight duties.

(*Below*) Snow ploughs, fitted to the front of 0–6–0 goods engines, clear the tracks in the north of England during the winter of 1941/2.

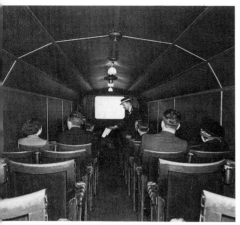

(*Above*) The interior of the cinema coach which was included in the LNER 'Flying Scotsman' express during the 1930s.

design that is little altered today. The GWR introduced in 1934 some successful single unit diesel railcars with a slick streamlined shape. They were built by AEC of Park Royal, who built London's buses, and the engine and certain internal fittings were the same in both road and rail vehicles. The LMSR experimented with a 750 hp three-coach diesel train in 1938 but the war put a halt to further experiments. The single most important step taken by any of the Big Four in developing non-steam traction took place in 1947 when the LMSR introduced No. 10000, Britain's first main line diesel-electric locomotive. It appeared only days before nationalization and we will return to its story later.

A problem common to all the Big Four railways was the increasing

(*Above*) Buffet cars were introduced in the 1930s for passengers who did not want a full meal. They remain popular today.

(*Below*) Pride of the Southern Electric fleet was the 'Brighton Belle'. This all-Pullman car train served refreshments at every seat and was introduced in 1933.

competition from road vehicles. The development of tram and bus services in the inner cities had nibbled away at suburban traffic for many years. Now there was a new threat. Hundreds of well-built lorries were being sold off cheaply by the army; men who would never otherwise have learnt to drive, but had been taught during the war, were out of work. Together men and machines were everywhere combining to form small haulage companies. Between 1920 and 1935 the number of road goods vehicles rose from 101,000 to 435,000. Railways were hindered by various laws passed in Victorian times to prevent them abusing the monopoly on transport they then

(*Above*) Colour photography came into popular use just in time to capture scenes of the Big Four. This is SR 'King Arthur' class 4–6–0 No. 739 *King Leodegrance* at Winchester with a Bournemouth express in April 1938.

(*Left*) Introduced in 1926, the SR 'Lord Nelson' class 4–6–0s were, for a time, the most powerful engines in the country. Soon after building, and before being filled with smoke deflectors, No. 859 *Lord Hood* races through Folkestone Warren with the 'Golden Arrow' boat train.

(*Above*) A train of the narrow gauge Lynton & Barnstaple Railway. The line served a remote part of Exmoor and closed in 1935; afterwards this locomotive, 2–4–2T No. 188 *Lew*, was sold to Brazil.

(*Above*) Easy does it, a powerful railway steam crane lifts the replica *North Star* over the top of 4–6–0 No. 6000 *King George V* at Swindon Works, GWR.

possessed. They had to accept all goods traffic that was offered to them regardless of whether or not it was economic to handle. Road operators in contrast could pick and choose only the most profitable customers and undercut the railways' charges as they liked.

Britain's railwaymen came out in support of the miners during the general strike of 1926. Goods traffic was lost to road haulage, never to be regained.

Some regulation of road transport was introduced by the government in the 1930s, but the Big Four had already met the challenge head-on. They had always owned large fleets of horse-drawn vehicles for local deliveries, but now they bought up competitors in the long-distance haulage business too. At nationalization in 1948 the Big Four owned 9,000 horses, 25,000 horse-drawn carts and wagons plus 11,000 road vehicles. They also purchased a half-share in a number of large bus fleets throughout the country.

Another area where railways were quick to seize control of the opposition was internal air services. In 1929 they took out parliamentary powers to operate aircraft and by 1934 Railway Air Services controlled virtually all passenger flights within Britain. All four railways had an interest, and Imperial Airways (the 1930s predecessor of British Airways) was a partner in the company.

Railway-owned shipping services continued as before. The first train ferries were introduced in 1924 on the Harwich to Zeebrugge route and followed by a Dover to Dunkerque service in 1936. Freight wagons were shunted directly onto the ferry boat which had rails laid on the deck. A passenger service called the 'Night Ferry' was run from Victoria to Paris via the Dunkerque route. It used specially adapted French Railways sleeping cars and operated from 1936 until 1980.

Although the Big Four sometimes co-operated with each other to fight a common foe their rivalry was often very real, and had spectacular results. When the LMSR and the LNER battled it out for the Anglo-Scottish traffic in the 1930s, the spirit of the old Race to the North was revived as speed records tumbled. The full story is told in the next chapter, but here is the 'curtain raiser'.

In 1928 the LNER decided to run its crack express, the 'Flying Scotsman', non-stop between King's Cross and Edinburgh. At 632 km (392.7 miles) this would be by far the longest non-stop railway journey in the world and splendid publicity for the LNER. There was, however, a problem. The run would take 8¼ hours and it was beyond the physical capability of one crew to drive or fire an engine for such a long time. Crews had to be changed half way, but how, without halting the train and losing the record?

Nigel Gresley, the LNER locomotive chief, came up with an answer which was as simple as it was ingenious. He designed new tenders for the most powerful Pacific engines. Each tender had a corridor running from end to end, connecting the cab to the first coach of the train. Two crews travelled on each train; one in the coaches and one on the footplate. At the halfway mark just north

Little and large of the LMSR. (*Above*) A tiny ex-North London Railway engine on the Hopton Incline – the steepest gradient in Britain worked by normal locomotives.
(*Below*) Mighty Pacific No. 6209 *Princess Beatrice.*

of York they changed places by walking through the tender — easy! The first non-stop 'Flying Scotsman' runs were scheduled for 1st May 1928. The eyes of the world were on the LNER. But the rival LMSR had plans to change this.

A mere three days before the LNER's event they staged a publicity spectacular of their own. Their 'Royal Scot' express usually ran from Euston to Glasgow with a portion for Edinburgh which was detached at Carstairs. On 28th April the LMSR split the train and ran it as two separate sections, both non-stop all the way. Two firemen, a driver and an inspector were wedged on to the footplate of an ageing and underpowered Compound 4-4-0 No. 1054. With

(*Above*)   LNER class 'B17' 4−6−0 No. 2833 *Kimbolton Castle* races through Brookmans Park in 1937. Nigel Gresley designed both locomotive and the teak-bodied coach behind it.

(*Left*)   The finest mixed traffic (passenger and freight) engines ever built were the LMSR class '5MT' 4−6−0s introduced in 1934. Several 'Black Fives' have been preserved, including No. 5025, restored to its LMSR livery and here at work in Scotland in 1984.

(*Above*)   A GWR classic 4–6–0 No. 6018 *King Henry VI* enters Exeter, St Davids with the 'Torbay Express' in October 1935. Chocolate and cream coaches, gleaming brass and a copper capped chimney – all the hallmarks of a Great Western express. No. 6018 was the last 'King' in service and was withdrawn in 1963.

coal piled as high as it would go in the tender, No. 1054 blasted away from Euston non-stop to Edinburgh, a distance of 643 km (399.7 miles). Minutes previously, the LMSR's mighty new 'Royal Scot' class 4-6-0 No. 6113 *Cameronian* had roared away in front of it, running without a halt over the 645.8 km (401.4 miles) to Glasgow.

Both runs were longer than that scheduled for the 'Flying Scotsman'. The LMSR had well and truly grabbed the LNER's glory. And although they were only one-off publicity stunts the LMSR non-stops went down in the record books. It was a great blow to the LNER's prestige, but one day they would get revenge!

(*Right*)   The SR 'Schools' class 4–4–0s were designed by R Maunsell and introduced in 1930. They were a cut-down version of his bigger engines, built to fit the narrow tunnels on the Hastings line. Three have been preserved. This is No. 926 *Repton* after restoration to its original colours in 1962 before it was sent to an American museum.

7 Thirties flyers

The 'World's Fastest Train', the Great Western Railway's 'Cheltenham Flyer' races through Tilehurst to the cheers of a group of schoolchildren in November 1934. The engine is 'Castle' class 4–6–0 No. 5000 *Launceston Castle*.

As the roaring twenties drew to a close, the Great Western Railway, ever publicity-conscious, produced a world beater. The 'Cheltenham Spa Express' was a modest enough train for the first 69 km (43 miles) of its journey. It passed unhurriedly through Gloucester, Stroud and Kemble on the edge of the Cotswolds before it reached Swindon. There it joined Brunel's great, straight and level main line for the final 124.4 km (77.3 miles) to London. In 1929 the GWR cut the timing for this stretch to 70 minutes, an average speed of 106.5 kph (66.2 mph) start-to-stop, and claimed the title of 'world's fastest daily train'! To the public it immediately become the 'Cheltenham Flyer'.

The Canadian Pacific Railroad briefly robbed the GWR of the title in 1931 but they regained supremacy a few months later. By September 1932 the 'Cheltenham Flyer', complete with large 'World's Fastest Train' headboard, was averaging 114.8 kph (71.4 mph) between Swindon and Paddington. On 6th June 1932 a deliberate record-breaking attempt took place when 'Castle' class 4-6-0 No. 5006 *Tregenna Castle* covered the ground in just 56¾

minutes at an average of 131.4 kph (81.7 mph) with 45 km (28 miles) taken at 145 to 148 kph (90 to 92 mph) It was a dramatic demonstration of the higher speeds possible with the bigger engines of the time. But the GWR's efforts were soon to be eclipsed totally by the traditional rivalry between the London, Midland & Scottish Railway and the London & North Eastern Railway.

By the mid-thirties diesel-electric traction was being used increasingly to speed up schedules on North American and German railways. The Germans had recently developed a network of fast diesel multiple-unit trains which had revolutionized services across the country. 'Fliegende Hamburger' was their German name which translated means 'Flying Hamburger' (it didn't sound funny then).

In Britain the directors of the LNER were keen to cut journey times on their East Coast main line between London King's Cross and the North. 'Flying Hamburger' units looked to be the answer

(*Above*)   'Castle' class 4–6–0 No. 5006 *Tregenna Castle*, hero of the 'Cheltenham Flyer' record run on 6th June 1932.

(*Left*)   The colour and glory of the Big Four.

1. LNER class 'A3' 4–6–2 No. 2750 *Papyrus*.
2. The beaver tail observation car at the rear of the LNER's Kings Cross-Edinburgh 'Coronation' express.
3. LMSR 'Royal Scot' 4–6–0 No. 6145 *The Duke of Wellington's Regiment (West Riding)* in original condition.
4. LMSR streamliner No. 6220 *Coronation* and the Euston-Glasgow 'Coronation Scot' express.
5. GWR 'Castle' class 4–6–0 No. 4088 *Dartmouth Castle*.
6. SR 'King Arthur' class 4–6–0 No. 769 *Sir Balan*.
7. SR 'Merchant Navy' class 4–6–2 No. 21C2 *Union Castle* and the Waterloo to Plymouth and Ilfracombe 'Devon Belle' Pullman train. Designed by Oliver Bulleid in 1941 these engines were nicknamed 'spam cans' because of their tinny appearance. All 30 were rebuilt and drastically altered during the late 1950s.

(*Right*) LNER class 'A4' No. 2509 *Silver Link* races out of London with the high speed demonstration run of the 'Silver Jubilee' on 27th September 1935.

(*Above*) Over a century of progress. A replica of the 1829-built *Rocket* stands next to LMSR 'Coronation' class 4–6–2 No. 6235 *City of Birmingham.*

(*Above*) In 1939 the 'Coronation Scot' train was sent to America for exhibition. This engine is actually No. 6229 *Duchess of Hamilton* pretending to be *Coronation.*

and German railway officials were asked to examine their suitability for use in this country. They came up with a projected schedule of 4¼ hours for the 431.7 km (268.3 miles) between London and Newcastle. This didn't completely impress the LNER men, who were sure it could be done even faster. The diesel units were also short trains with relatively cramped accommodation and catering which consisted only of a cold buffet. Not quite the luxury image the LNER wanted to go with its fast timings.

Sir Nigel Gresley, the LNER's Chief Mechanical Engineer, also believed steam could do better. On 30th November 1934 he ran a high speed test train from London to Leeds and back. Headed by his famous Pacific No. 4472 *Flying Scotsman* and with the fiery driver Bill Sparshatt in control, the train was pushed up to the magic 160 kph (100 mph) figure on the return journey. Unlike *City of Truro's* controversial 'ton' in 1904 no one could argue with this record, for included in the train was a dynamometer car (in effect a mobile laboratory packed with scientific instruments to record every detail of the run). The 160 kph (100 mph) top speed was good publicity but even more significant was the fact that over 402.2 km (250 miles) of the day's run had been covered at an average of 128.7 kph (80 mph).

Six months later, on 5th March 1935, another Gresley engine, No. 2750 *Papyrus* fully earned its racehorse name when it knocked the diesel men's schedules sideways. Hauling a six-coach train and with Driver Sparshatt once more in charge, *Papyrus* raced from King's Cross to Newcastle in 3 hours 57 minutes, then hurtled back to London in five minutes less. And down the LNER's traditional race track, Stoke Bank between Grantham and Peterborough, it was hammered up to a new high of 173.8 kph (108 mph). It would be over twenty-five more years before diesels finally outshone steam on the East Coast route.

(*Left*) Inside the beaver-tail observation car carried at the rear of the LNER 'Coronation' express.

(*Above*) The fastest steam engine in the world. LNER 4–6–2 No. 4468 *Mallard*, in 1963.

So steam was to head Britain's first purpose built high-speed train on a superfast four-hour London to Newcastle schedule. And what a train! Named the 'Silver Jubilee' after the royal anniversary that year, it too was a headline grabber from the start. To haul it Gresley had designed a powerful new streamlined Pacific, the 'A4' class. The wedge-fronted design owed something to the style of contemporary racing cars and was aimed at reducing wind resistance at speed. The locomotive wheels were partly covered by steel casing and similar panels extended below the carriage bodies. Gaps between the coach ends were sealed off with rubber to make the complete train as tight and fast a unit as possible. Inside, the coaches were the last word in elegant, comfortable, modern design. Externally the whole train was painted silver grey from end to end.

Three days before the 'Silver Jubilee' commenced public running, the LNER staged a trial to demonstrate its prowess. On 27th September 1935 the first of the 'A4s', No. 2509 *Silver Link*, stormed out of King's Cross with a party of specially invited guests and reporters aboard. The engine men had been told to go for it, and this they did, with a vengeance! *Silver Link* had scarcely cleared the London suburbs before it was up to 160 kph (100 mph), a speed it maintained for over 40.2 consecutive kilometres (25 miles). Then it effortlessly smashed *Papyrus's* record with a maximum speed of 181 kph (112½ mph). And it wasn't a fluke. *Silver Link* went on to head the 'Silver Jubilee' every day for its first fortnight of regular public service, without losing a minute on the exacting timings.

More 'A4s' were built, and in August the next year No. 2512 *Silver Fox* was inched past *Silver Link's* record to a new high of 181.8 kph (113 mph). Unfortunately the locomotive had been hammered too fiercely up one side of the Stoke Bank to get a good run down the other, and overheating cylinders caused the crew to throw on the brakes almost at once. Steam and disintegrating metal

(*Above*) The corridor tender fitted to LNER engines working long non-stop runs.

(*Left*) A very rare colour photograph of LNER No. 2509 *Silver Link* at Grantham in June 1937 while working the 'Flying Scotsman' express.

(*Above*) Even rarer is this colour shot of No. 4468 *Mallard* on 3rd July 1938 – the day it took the world speed record for a steam locomotive.

(*Left*) Probably the most famous locomotive in the world. LNER 4–6–2 No. 4472 *Flying Scotsman* was built in 1922 and is still steaming well. Since 1963 it has been preserved and, apart from a spell in America, has run regular trips for enthusiasts. This is a recent picture.

(*Right*) Another thirties flyer that is still going strong is *Duchess of Hamilton*, the engine that went to America pretending to be *Coronation* in 1939. The streamlined casing was later removed from all the LMSR Pacifics and in their final years of service they looked like this. When it was first preserved, *Duchess of Hamilton* was exhibited in a holiday camp. Now it steams again leaving York with an excursion for railway enthusiasts.

(*Above*) Star of the 1936 non-stop Euston to Glasgow runs was LMSR 'Princess Royal' class 4–6–2 No. 6201 *Princess Elizabeth*.

(*Right*) Although the first LMSR streamliners that worked the 'Coronation Scot' express were painted blue, five others were turned out in crimson lake with gold lining. This rare shot is a frame from a railway enthusiast's cine-film of No. 6227 *Duchess of Devonshire* leaving Euston in 1938.

sprayed everywhere and *Silver Fox* limped on to London at a very much slower pace.

In the autumn of 1936 the LNER announced that they were going to introduce another fully streamlined train similar to the 'Silver Jubilee'. It would operate between King's Cross and Edinburgh, taking only 6 hours for the 631.8 km (392.7 miles). The LMSR had to answer the challenge on its rival West Coast main line. An immediate response was two special non-stop Euston to Glasgow return runs headed by Pacific No. 6201 *Princess Elizabeth*. Record timings of 5 hours 53 minutes and 5 hours 44 minutes for the 645.8 km (401.4 miles) proved that the LMSR could run to a 6-hour schedule as well. It looked as if the battle was on.

The following year, 1937, was coronation year for King George VI, and both the new trains took appropriate names. The LNER 'Coronation' looked every inch a winner. It was fully streamlined with a brand new 'A4' at the head and decked out in garter blue livery. At the rear was an observation car with wide glass windows all round. Its distinctive sloping 'beaver tail' shape complemented the streamlined appearance of the whole train and for a 1/- (5p) supplement passengers could sit in comfortable armchairs and enjoy panoramic views. Externally the LMSR train, called the 'Coronation Scot' looked good too. Sir William Stanier (Gresley's equivalent on the LMSR) had also designed a class of massive streamlined Pacifics to haul the train and the colour scheme, blue and silver, was similar. But inside, the coaches were disappointingly ordinary and hardly compared with the plush of the 'Coronation'. Despite the magnificent trial runs of the previous year, the 'Coronation Scot' was timed to take 6½ hours from London to Glasgow. But the LMSR had one ace to play, or so it thought. Copying the LNER, officials arranged a special trip for the press prior to the 'Coronation Scot' commencing regular operation. And, without announcing it in advance, they resolved to better the LNER's still standing speed record of 181.8 kph (113 mph)

Unfortunately the LMSR didn't have a convenient race track section like the LNER. A 10.4 km (6.5 mile) downhill stretch

(*Above*) The LMSR 'Coronation Scot' express thunders through Hemel Hempstead on 22nd March 1938. At its head is the first of Stanier's streamlined Pacifics, No. 6220 *Coronation*.

northbound from Whitmore near Crewe was the best they could manage. On 29th June 1937 locomotive No. 6220 *Coronation* thrashed out of Euston on what turned out to be the railway equal to a 'white knuckle ride'. Urged on by officials riding on the footplate, Driver Clarke opened the regulator wide as *Coronation* flew down from Whitmore. Only 3 km (2 miles) from Crewe station itself *Coronation* hit its top speed. The LMSR top brass later trumpeted a new record of 183.4 kph (114 mph) based on the engine's speedometer read-out, but many expert observers using stop watches on the train reckoned it was at best a dead heat with *Silver Fox*. Whatever the maximum, *Coronation* was still doing 92 kph (57 mph) as it hit the maze of crossover tracks outside Crewe station. White-faced footplate staff hung on for dear life, crockery cascaded in a crashing heap to the floor of the dining car and passengers tumbled into each other as, by a miracle, *Coronation* rode the points and stayed upright!

Gresley watched, and determined to settle things once and for all. He would not only put the record out of the LMSR's reach but also beat the Germans, who had worked a steam locomotive up to 200 kph (124½ mph) in 1936. On 3rd July 1938 he staged what were officially termed braking trials down the Stoke Bank racetrack. To head a seven-coach train weighing 240 tons he chose his newest 'A4' No. 4468 *Mallard*, which was only a few months old. Included in the train was the dynamometer car; Gresley wanted no room for doubt. Joe Duddington, a fearless Yorkshireman, was chosen to drive *Mallard* on a day that would go down in history.

Mallard started from Barkston, just north of Grantham, and took Stoke Bank at a run. It was doing 119 kph (74 mph) at the top then streaked away down the other side. For 5 km (3 miles) the garter blue streamlined engine held 193 kph (120 mph) and briefly, but unarguably, it touched 202.7 kph (126 mph). The world speed record for steam was *Mallard's* and would remain so for all time!

Just over a year later the Second World War broke out and the racing stopped. The 'Silver Jubilee', 'Coronation' and 'Coronation Scot' would never reappear. But one day there would be a train that could equal *Mallard's* record every day.

(*Above*) The 100th Gresley Pacific was built in 1937 and named after its designer. No. 4498 *Sir Nigel Gresley* is now preserved.

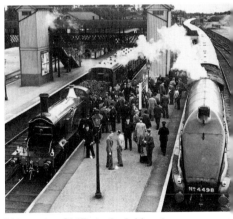

(*Above*) GNR 4–2–2 No. 1 and LNER 4–6–2 No. 4498 *Sir Nigel Gresley* pose together at Stevenage with trains representing the 'Flying Scotsman' of 1888 and 1938 respectively.

8 Railway at war

On Sunday 3rd September 1939 radios throughout Great Britain broadcast the message that everyone had long been dreading, the country was once more at war with Germany. It was far from unexpected. The Railway Executive Committee had been reformed two days earlier and already was preparing its plans to run the Big Four and London Transport from the safety of a bomb-proof shelter deep below the streets of London. If the First World War had severely tested the strength of Britain's railway system, then this second great conflict would strain its every sinew to breaking point.

The first task was immediate and already underway when the wirelesses crackled out their dramatic message. Evacuation! Aircraft had improved out of all recognition since the previous war, particularly bombers. The world had just seen the German air force, the Luftwaffe, at work ruthlessly bombing defenceless cities and slaughtering unarmed civilians during the Spanish Civil War. No one was under any illusions about the fate that lay ahead for Britain.

So began the rush to evacuate thousands of women and children, the sick and the elderly too, from the great industrial cities where bombing was expected to be heaviest. This mass exodus had been planned well in advance and went without a hitch. During the first weekend in September a total of 1,334,358 people in 3,823 special trains were taken out of the danger areas to the safety of the countryside. Known as evacuees, the children made a sorry sight as they waited on the crowded platforms for their trains to arrive. Each child clutched its gas mask, a favourite toy and a tiny suitcase or bundle containing a few clean clothes. Firmly tied to every child's coat was a label bearing its name and address in case it got lost or separated from the accompanying mother or schoolteacher.

From London it was not just people that were being removed. The nation's art treasures were sent away by train to be hidden deep underground in the Welsh mountains. There they were joined by the gold from the vaults of the Bank of England.

At the same time as the railways were coping with a million evacuees they were also transporting the British Expeditionary Force to Southampton. Clickety-clacking over the same route as their fathers in 1914, the troops travelled in a procession of special trains that eventually wound their way into the docks where the boats for France were waiting.

For the second time in 25 years armoured trains are built as a precaution against the invasion of Britain. This was 'one of many stationed on the East Coast' at the beginning of the war.

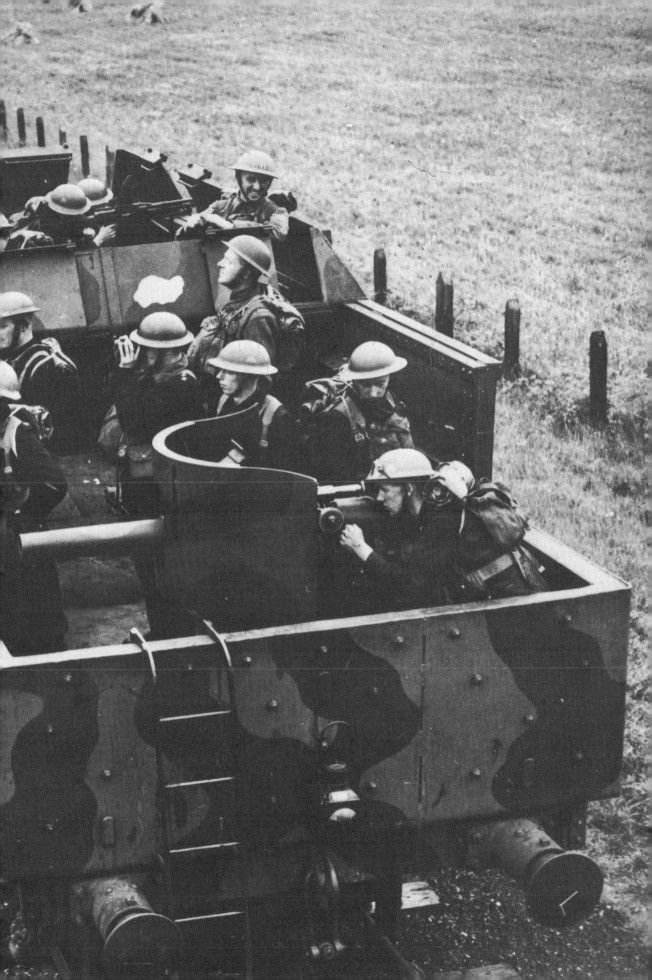

By late October everyone, soldiers and civilians alike, was poised for battle; and nothing happened! Hitler's forces had over-run Poland in a matter of days but then they stopped. The winter months of 1939–40 were the time of the 'phoney war'. Evacuees, bored by life with strange families in the unaccustomed peace and quiet of the countryside, began to drift back into the cities. Then in April 1940 Germany unleashed its blitzkreig or lightning war on Norway and Holland, followed quickly by an all-out attack on Belgium and France. Within weeks it was over and the BEF itself was being evacuated from the beaches of Dunkerque. Over 600 special trains were run during May, made up of anything that would turn a wheel. They conveyed more than 319,000 weary or injured soldiers returning from the Dover area to camps and hospitals across Britain.

Life for the entire population of Britain would be very different this time from the experience of 1914–18. Every man, woman and child in the country was as firmly in the Front Line as the soldiers themselves. And railway staff were in it up to the hilt. From the very beginning of the war the number of passenger trains was cut drastically and freight given priority. Restaurant cars disappeared. Two or even three passenger services were sometimes combined into one immense train with up to 26 coaches and hauled by a single engine. At King's Cross station the first coach of such a train would actually be in Gasworks Tunnel many metres beyond the end of the platform. To start the train a member of staff had to walk down the track and into the pitch black tunnel to give the driver the right away.

All long-distance trains were crowded beyond belief with members of the armed forces travelling to camp or home on leave. Travel for pleasure was all but barred. Not that anyone had much

(*Above*) Children evacuated from London get a helping hand from a cheerful LNER porter in 1940.

(*Right*) Two of the US Army Transportation Corps S160 2–8–0s double head a freight at Wootton Bassett in 1943. These engines went to Europe after 'D' Day and were to be seen in many European countries until recently.

spare time nor were there many places to visit. Long sections of the coastline were out of bounds with barbed wire standing silent guard against invasion on beaches where once only sandcastles had been built. The polite notices of 1914–18 had given way to strident propaganda. 'Is your journey really necessary,' shouted the posters. 'Give your seat to a shell.' There was a total blackout of all strong illumination at night, to prevent enemy bombers identifying their targets. Running a railway in these conditions was extremely difficult and hazardous. Lighting in freight yards and at stations was virtually non-existent. Platform edges were whitewashed to show passengers where they were and stop them stumbling onto the tracks. Train lights were reduced to the bare minimum and windows blacked out leaving only a small peephole for passengers to peer through. Sheeting was fixed over steam locomotive cabs to conceal the glow of the fire — an easy mark for German aircraft. Other air raid precautions included removing all the glass panes from the massive overall roofs of stations such as St Pancras and York.

Over 109,000 railway staff joined the armed forces, and tragically nearly 3,500 died. But those who were directed to stay behind frequently faced danger every bit as real as those who went into battle. In the five and a half years of war there were 9,239 incidents where railway property was damaged by enemy action, and 250 of these caused sufficient damage to take a week or more to repair. Bombs rained down without mercy on stations big and small, signal-boxes, engine sheds, tunnels, bridges and trains. Air raids started with the London blitz of autumn 1940 and soon spread to other inland cities such as Coventry, then to the ports of Liverpool, Plymouth and Portsmouth. During a savage night attack on Barrow-in-Furness in 1941 the whole station was destroyed. Nearby, old *Coppernob*, an ancient Furness Railway engine, was rudely awakened from its slumbers as the glass of the exhibition hall in which it slept was blown to smithereens. But *Coppernob* survived and today is proudly on show at the National Railway Museum in York. Take a look at the jagged holes in its boiler and great brass firebox; that's where the blast ripped into it on a night to remember in 1941.

Even as the war neared its end London continued to be attacked. In 1944 and 1945 over 1,400 V1 and V2 rocket bombs, the first ever used in modern warfare, fell on to railway property, more than

(*Above*) Stanier's LMSR class '8F' 2–8–0 design was adopted for War Department needs.

(*Above*) Women at work building Lancaster bombers at Derby works, LMSR.

(*Above*) Travelling by rail to victory. A train of tanks during the build-up to 'D' Day.

100 of them scoring direct hits on vital equipment. Destruction to locomotives and rolling stock too was heavy. Eight steam locomotives, 637 carriages and 3,321 wagons were totally destroyed during the war. About 500, 13,000 and 20,000 of each were damaged.

Sadly, 395 railway staff were killed on duty and 2,444 injured during enemy attacks. Very many showed great courage while going about their everyday duties. One was Norman Tunna, a shunter in the GWR freight yard at Birkenhead. During a heavy air raid on the nearby Liverpool Docks one night, Mr Tunna continued to work as normal. He had just completed marshalling a long train containing many 250 lb bombs when he discovered two German firebombs had fallen into one of the wagons. They had landed on a tarpaulin cover and set it alight. Soon the lot would go up! Without thought for his own safety Mr Tunna raced to fetch buckets of water to quench the fire, but they had no effect. Then he tore off the blazing sheet with his bare hands and managed to remove one of the firebombs. Leaping on to the wagon he found the other firebomb was wedged between two of the 250 pounders. Using his long shunter's pole he managed to prise the firebomb out and throw it to the ground. The danger was not past yet, as the British bombs were still very hot. Mr Tunna stayed in the wagon hosing them down with cold water until at last all danger of explosion had passed. But for his heroism the full trainload of bombs would have exploded, causing tremendous damage and a terrific loss of life. Norman Tunna was awarded the George Cross and today a diesel locomotive proudly bears his name.

Perhaps it was a desire to hit back at the enemy that caused one elderly locomotive to bring down a German plane. On the morning of 28th November 1942, the Southern Railway's Class D3 0-4-4T No. 2365 was pottering contentedly over Romney Marsh with a local train. Suddenly a lone enemy aircraft dived out of the sky to attack at low level, raking locomotive and coaches with machine gun fire. Now No. 2365 was 50 years old and many years ago had been named *Victoria*; she wasn't going to stand for such rude treatment of a lady! As the plane roared overhead her boiler exploded

(*Above*) Southampton was hit hard by air-raids. This is the ruined Central station on 22nd June 1941.

(*Above*) Bomb damage to St Pancras station.

(*Right*) 'Austerity' class 2–8–0s and 2–10–0s were built in large numbers for the War Department after 1943. A total of 758 were eventually taken over by British Railways after the war's end. This is No. 90074 taking water at West Hartlepool one day before steam finished there in September 1967.

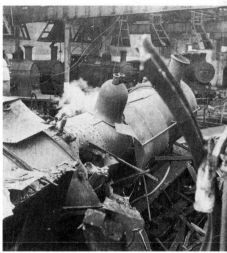

(*Left*) Not a real battle. Soldiers practise hand-to-hand combat around Scholes signalbox in Yorkshire, July 1941.

(*Above*) Fratton depot after a direct hit on 10th January 1941.

(*Above*) A bomb disposal squad heave an unexploded German bomb on to a four-wheeled truck at Peckham Rye.

and either the uprush of steam or a fragment of metal hit the aircraft, which crashed killing its pilot.

The majority of ex-main-line British locomotives sent abroad during the Second World War went to the Middle East. Some, the old Great Central Railway 2-8-0s, had been called up once before; this time they did not return. In the months prior to D-Day, however, 756 2-8-0 freight locomotives classified S160 were shipped over from America by the USA Transportation Corps. Although destined for Europe after the invasion, nearly 400 were used for a time on the hard-pressed railways of Britain. They were tough, rugged locomotives and long after the war's end could still be seen on the railways of many East European countries.

The LMS Class 8F 2-8-0 and two very basic new designs of 'Austerity' 2-8-0 and 2-10-0 were adopted as the standard War Department engines. Once again all the railway workshops were busy making bombs, guns, landing craft and tanks instead of engines.

By the spring of 1945 it was obvious the war was nearly over. A general election was called and a Labour government committed to nationalization was returned to parliament. Before he stood down, Prime Minister Winston Churchill, who had seen Britain though the dark years of war, expressed his gratitude to the railways in a personal message. Another came from General Eisenhower who had commanded the Allied Forces at D-Day. He gave his thanks for their efforts in the huge task of transporting men and materials in preparation for the invasion.

Railwaymen and women of every grade had struggled for nearly six years to keep Britain moving despite the most terrible conditions imaginable. Troops, guns, tanks or bombs, they carried everything that was given them. Enemy attacks never halted the trains for long. This all-out effort had left its mark, however, and locomotives,

(*Above*)   After the war there was a shortage of coal and a number of locomotives were fitted to burn oil instead. This is GWR 'Hall' Class 4–6–0 No. 5955 *Garth Hall*. Note the oil tank in the tender's coal space.

(*Left*)   Children being evacuated by train at the beginning of the war.

(*Right*)   The rivals. LMSR 4–6–2 No. 6256 *Sir William A Stanier FRS* and Britain's first main line diesel-electric No. 10000 on display at Euston, 18th December 1947.

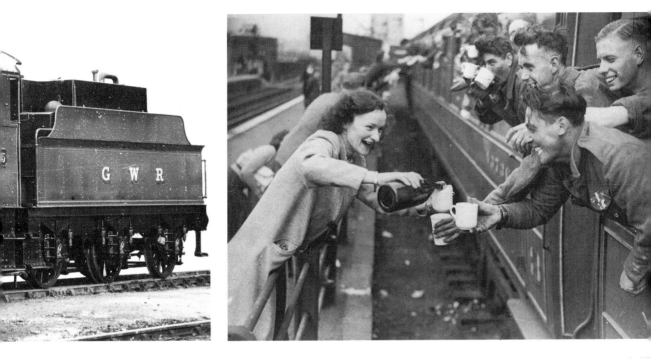

carriages and track were all badly run-down; there simply hadn't been time for regular overhauls or repairs. But without their efforts the war might not have been won. As one railway historian has put it, 'the effort of the British railways over the years 1940–45 represented the greatest achievement in railway transportation in the history of the world'.

The Railway Executive Committee continued to control the operations of the Big Four until 6th August 1947 when the Act of Parliament nationalizing them was passed. On 1st January 1948 Britain's railways became British Railways.

(*Above*)   A different group of evacuees – the British Expeditionary Force, recently rescued from the beaches of Dunkirk, are taken away from the Dover area by special trains in June 1940.

9 British Railways

At first, British Railways' express engines were painted blue. This is 'Merchant Navy' Class 4–6–2 No. 35024 *East Asiatic Company* at Waterloo in June 1949. In its train is a Pullman car conveying Princess Elizabeth.

At midnight on 31st December 1947, steam locomotives up and down the country sounded their whistles in a time-honoured greeting to the new year. But 1948 was not to be like previous years, for now the railways were nationalized, owned by the government of Great Britain on behalf of its people. The task of unifying the system, tackled half-heartedly in 1923, was finally complete. A body entitled the British Transport Commission (BTC) was set up to oversee all the newly nationalized transport systems. These included docks, inland waterways and road haulage as well as railways. Beneath it a Railway Executive controlled the daily running of the new organization known simply as British Railways, BR for short.

(*Left*) Early days of BR. The arrival of the 'Irish Mail' at Euston, 6.35am on 27th May 1948. Both locomotives are rebuilt 'Royal Scot' 4–6–0s.

(*Above*) Painters at Crewe Works put the finishing touches to 4–6–2 No. 46241 *City of Edinburgh* in its new British Railways livery, May 1948.

(*Below*) The Locomotive Exchanges, 1948, London Midland Region Pacific No. 46236 *City of Bradford* leaves Waterloo with the 10.50am to Exeter. The tender was specially fitted for this working. No. 46236 was once streamlined – you can tell by the slope to the top of the smokebox.

In place of the Big Four's boundaries, the network was divided into six regions. These regions and the areas they covered were: Western Region (former GWR lines); Southern Region (former Southern Railway lines); London Midland Region (the former LMSR lines from Carlisle southwards); Eastern Region (the southern half of the LNER); North Eastern Region (the North Eastern area of the LNER) and a Scottish Region which took in everything north of the Border. Each region was allocated a different distinguishing colour to use on station signs, staff uniform badges and publicity material. For the Western the colour was chocolate; it was green for the Southern, maroon for the London Midland, dark blue for the Eastern, orange for the North Eastern, and light blue for the Scottish Region.

New liveries were also needed for locomotives and rolling stock,

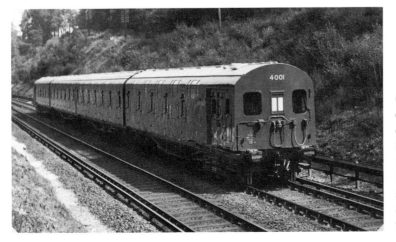

(*Left*) In steam days engines were tested at the Rugby Testing Station which was completed in 1948. A technician is monitoring the performance of a 'Black Five'.

(*Above*) A rare shot of No. 36001, Bulleid's revolutionary 'Leader' class engine, during one of its trial runs.

(*Above*) Old-style freight handling in 1951.

(*Left*) Another Bulleid experiment was a double decker train for the Southern Region's Dartford commuter route introduced on 2nd November 1949. Two 4 car sets were built, capable of carrying 1104 passengers in total.

and 30 days after nationalization senior officials of BR were the judges in an unusual beauty competition held at Kensington, when four Class 5MT 4-6-0s were paraded up and down for their inspection. Each was painted in a different colour: three in the differing shades of green used by the GWR, SR and LNER, and one in the black of the pre-grouping London & North Western Railway. No decision was taken immediately. Another series of experimental colours was applied to locomotives in service, and the public were asked to give their opinion on them. Express passenger engines were deep blue, ordinary passenger engines were painted a bright (very bright) apple green and the rest were black. A lighter shade of blue was then tried out, but none of the new colour schemes seems to have clicked with the passengers. Eventually it was decided to paint all passenger engines in deep brunswick green, lined out in orange and black — the colours of the GWR. All other steam locomotives would be black, as would the few diesels and electrics.

A new colour scheme for main line passenger coaches was also

fixed. This was to be a rather startling combination officially known as carmine and cream, but usually referred to as blood and custard. Suburban coaches were to be red, excepting SR electric units which would be green. Matching colours they were not!

Gradually the brave new colours began to appear on locomotives, coaches, badges and posters. But in some ways it was an empty gesture to an uncertain future. BR had inherited all the problems of four railways worn out by six years of unsparing effort during the war. In Europe the railways had suffered too, far worse than in Britain. Now, however, they were rebuilding at an incredible pace helped by money from America. Their systems had been so bombed and battered into the ground that it was easier to start from scratch. Everything was new and the opportunity was being grasped to electrify the main lines with the most sophisticated modern equipment.

In Britain the railways had to patch up as best they could. And they were not alone. It was a time of austerity, and a cold, grey, drabness affected everyone. Clothes, meat and sweets were still rationed as they had been during the war. Industry too was rationed, starved of raw materials as it tried to re-gear itself to peacetime production. There was a shortage of coal. In 1946 the government had ordered the railways to convert 1,200 locomotives to burn oil instead. No sooner had they started, than a financial crisis pushed

(*Above*) First of the standard engines, 4–6–2 No. 70000 *Britannia*, brand new in 1951.

(*Above*) No. 75000, the first of the standard class '4MT' 4–6–0s, under construction at Swindon Works in May 1951.

(*Left*) Built in 1954, No. 71000 *Duke of Gloucester* was intended to be the first of a fleet of powerful new express engines. The modernization plan changed all that. Photographed leaving Euston with the 'Mid-day Scot' in 1957, No. 71000 had only five years' service left.

up the price of oil and the scheme was abandoned. In these circumstances it is hardly suprising that there was little enthusiasm for ambitious plans to use diesel locomotives rather than steam.

On 1st January 1948 BR took over 20,023 steam locomotives, 53 diesel locomotives (mainly shunters), 40 diesel railcars, 16 electric locomotives, and 2,006 electric train vehicles. The steam locomotives were made up of no less than 448 different types, some of which were 70 years old. Engines which had been withdrawn for scrapping before the war had been reprieved and put back into service to help the all-out effort. Many locomotives were now life-expired and there was a terrific backlog of maintenance.

A few new locomotive types were designed by the Big Four in the run up to nationalization; all except one followed conventional lines. The joker in the pack was the *Leader*, brainchild of Oliver Bulleid, the Southern Railway's Chief Mechanical Engineer. This was a bizarre machine quite unlike any previous steam locomotive. It was square-shaped, with a cab at each end, and ran on two six-wheeled bogies each powered by a three-cylinder engine. The fireman was located in a centrally placed cabin, to one side of the

(*Above*)   Standard class '5MT' 4–6–0 No. 73125. These engines were based on the LMSR 'Black Fives'.

(*Above*)   One of the first diesel multiple unit trains runs through the Lake District in 1954. With their wide windows and panoramic views they were an instant hit with the public.

(*Left*)   The funeral train of King George VI at Paddington, 15th February 1952.

(*Above*) The bus-type seating inside one of the new diesel trains.

(*Above*) A freight train hauled by class 'EM1' locomotive No. 26022 approaches the level crossing at Torside on the newly-electrified Woodhead route.

boiler, which quickly became a cauldron of heat and dust. *Leader* had been commissioned originally by the Southern Railway, but when No. 36001 finally appeared two years later, the Railway Executive were in charge and viewed this complicated monstrosity with dismay. After a few troublesome trials it was quietly scrapped. The *Leader* was historically significant though because it represented the last serious attempt to rethink steam locomotive design in this country. Soon afterwards Bulleid left BR for Ireland, where he built a locomotive which ran on peat.

Simplicity was to be the keynote of BR's new locomotives; and they would be steam. R A Riddles of the LMSR was appointed to head a team of designers from the old Big Four companies. Comparative trials were held in 1948, when locomotives were exchanged between regions to assess their performance on different routes. The trials were carefully observed and data obtained in an effort to extract the best from each design. Eventually it was decided to build twelve different types of standard engine for both passenger and freight duties. They would work over all six regions, making it possible to withdraw the most antique locomotives.

Riddles had designed the plain, 'Austerity', wartime engines for the Ministry of Supply. He had also admired the rugged American S160s during their brief stay in this country. To some degree his new standard locomotives copied this straightforward, no-nonsense approach. They were essentially get-at-able engines and easy to maintain. True this meant raising the running plate high above the wheels and leaving more pipework outside than was usual in British designs. But, for the shed staff, the 'standards' were easier to service than many a pretty engine which had all its important working bits tucked away where no one could reach them.

No. 70000, the first of the standard engines, appeared early in 1951 and was named *Britannia* at Marylebone on 30th January. A total of 55 'Britannias' were built, and they took on all but the heaviest express passenger trains. Other standard classes were intended for lighter cross-country and branch line trains. Several types were very similar to those built by the LMSR just after the war. As both Riddles and H G Ivatt, one of his principal designers, were former LMSR men perhaps this wasn't surprising! The twelfth design to appear was a 2-10-0 freight engine. Classified '9F', these were excellent free-steaming machines capable of hauling the heaviest freight trains.

The heavy traffic and enforced lack of maintenance during the war had left main line track in a poor state, and it was a considerable time before fast running could be resumed. By 1953, however, the East Coast once again had a fast non-stop Anglo-Scottish express. Called the 'Elizabethan' in honour of our Queen's coronation that year, it was timed at 6¾ hours between King's Cross and Edinburgh. Although they were nearly twenty years old, it was Gresley's streamlined 'A4' Pacifics that worked the service. They were fitted with corridor tenders and regularly put up performances equal to their pre-war running.

In 1959, with a famous hell-for-leather driver called Bill Hoole at the regulator on his last run before retirement, 'A4' No. 60007 *Sir Nigel Gresley* hit 180 kph (112 mph) down Stoke Bank with a special train for the Stephenson Locomotive Society. It was the highest post-war speed achieved with steam, and legend has it that Bill Hoole was well on his way to smashing *Mallard's* record before senior officials on the footplate said 'no'.

By the mid-1950s all the big pre-war express passenger engines seemed to be getting their second wind. Steam was enjoying an Indian summer. But these ageing locomotives could not be expected to last for ever. A new standard Pacific, similar to the 'Britannias' in appearance but much more powerful, was designed to replace them. The prototype, No. 71000, emerged from Crewe Works in 1954 and was named *Duke of Gloucester*. It was intended to be the first of many near-identical engines but, in fact, *Duke of Gloucester* was destined to mark the end of a noble line.

Although each of the Big Four had dabbled with diesels, the LMSR can claim to have done the real pioneering work. In the last month of their existence, on 12th December 1947, the LMSR unveiled No. 10000 — Britain's first main line diesel-electric locomotive. Built at Derby, to the design of H G Ivatt working in close collaboration with the private firm of English Electric, the new locomotive was certainly an impressive sight. But, although it weighed a hefty 127 tons, only 1,600 hp was contained under its bulbous-nosed American-style body. A twin, No. 10001, arrived in 1948 and for many years the two ran in multiple, coupled together but with only one crew driving from the leading engine — a more economical arrangement than double-headed steam engines.

The Southern Railway had started design work on a trio of main line diesels in 1946 but it was 1951 before the first two appeared. Nos. 10201 and 10202 were joined by a third, slightly more powerful, sister in 1954. This locomotive, No. 10203, had a 2,000 hp engine designed by English Electric. A mere four years later a virtually identical engine would be used in the English Electric Type 4s, the first main line diesel-electric locomotives to be

(*Above*) Ordered by the GWR in the 1940s, 3,000 hp gas turbine No. 18100 finally arrived from Metropolitan Vickers in December 1951. It ran passenger service until 1958 before being converted to an electric locomotive.

(*Above*) One of the three Southern Railway-designed diesel-electrics, No. 10202, working on the London Midland Region.

(*Above*) Rebuilt 'Patriot' class 4–6–0 No. 45531 *Sir Frederick Harrison* just out of the Derby paint shop in 1948. It is painted in the rather lurid, and short-lived, experimental apple green livery.

built in large numbers. Slowly, the diesel era was dawning!

At nationalization only 1,454 km (904 miles) of route were electrified. Most of this was on the Southern which represented the only real electric railway system. The rest was made up of odd suburban lines in the Wirral, Manchester, North London and other places. Certain schemes begun before the war and then abandoned for obvious reasons were gradually finished. Electric working was started between Liverpool Street and Shenfield on September 1949. Another pre-war LNER project was finally completed on 3rd June, 1954. This was the electrification of the route over the Pennines between Manchester, Sheffield and Wath which carried very heavy freight traffic. A 1,500 volt dc overhead wire system was used, with LNER-design locomotives of 1,868 and 2,490 hp hauling both passenger and freight trains. It was the first time electric locomotives had been employed on BR passenger duties. At Woodhead a completely new tunnel was cut to take the overhead equipment and the electric locomotives sailed through. It was clean and efficient work and a dramatic contrast to the choking blackness in the old tunnels during steam days. The Woodhead electrification pointed to the future.

There were over 40,000 passenger coaches on BR in 1948. Like the locomotives, many were long past retiring age. More than 1,000 had wooden bodies and some were still gas-lit. Moves were made to standardize coaching stock in the same way as locomotives. A new steel-bodied design which borrowed many features from the best LMSR coaches was evolved. Known as the Mark I, the first example appeared in 1951 and thousands were built over the next fifteen years.

Nearly ten years after the end of the Second World War, British Railways, through no fault of its own, lagged behind the best railways in Europe. It was basically a steam-operated system and modernization was haphazard. At York for instance new electric colour-light signalling contrasted oddly with a major passenger station still using gas lighting. In 1952 the BTC had stated it was to spend half-a-million pounds on new diesel trains to replace ageing steam stock on branch lines and secondary routes. All good stuff, but something more comprehensive was needed.

On 24th January 1955, Sir Brian Robertson, Chairman of the BTC, announced a £1,200 million scheme for the modernization and re-equipment of British Railways. The money was to be spent on improving track, introducing new signalling and rebuilding stations. Freight wagons with continuous brakes for fast running would be designed. There would be more new carriages. But for many people it was the intended changes in motive power which were the most important. The plan called for long-term widespread electrification of main line and suburban routes. As a stop-gap diesels were to take over from steam, although it was intended that about 7,000 steam locomotives would remain by 1970. After the completion of existing orders within the next few years, however, no new steam locomotives were to be built. Steam's long journey that had begun with Trevithick's Penydarren engine, over 150 years previously, was nearly ended.

(*Above*) Inside the cab of class 'EM2' electric locomotive No. 27004 *Juno* on the Woodhead route in 1954. This engine was sold to Dutch Railways some years ago.

(*Below*) The colours of BR in the mid 1950s; No. 60007 *Sir Nigel Gresley* is in lined-out Brunswick green and the coaches are painted 'blood and custard'.

10 Changing trains

During the first few years following the announcement of the modernization plan progress was sure, but it was also slow. In 1955 British Railways possessed only 456 diesels, mainly shunters, compared to 17,955 steam engines. Its workshops and those of most of the private builders were geared to producing steam rather than diesel locomotives. Political considerations would not allow BR to buy diesels from America, where designs were far advanced and steam virtually eliminated. The only answer was to go back to the drawing board.

A pilot scheme was decided upon; 174 diesels of various designs in three power ranges between 800 and 2,000 hp were to be ordered from different manufacturers. Each type would then be put through extensive tests and the best designs identified before placing large

The first main line diesels to be built in large numbers were the English Electric Type 4s. This is the second example, No. D201, at the head of the 'Master Cutler' Pullman, in September 1958.

(*Right*) End of an era. *Evening Star* was the last steam locomotive to be built by British Railways. It ran for only five years before being preserved.

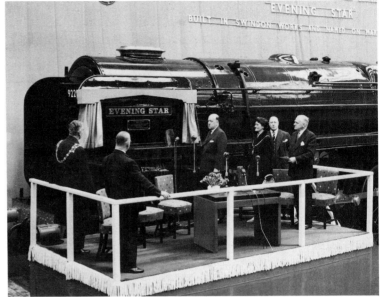

(*Above*) Once she was the pride of the LMSR. Now No. 46204 *Princess Louise* is cut and hammered into scrap metal at Crewe works, 17th April 1962.

(*Below*) Racing into a new age. One of the Western Region's diesel-hydraulics, No. D805 *Benbow*, speeds through Sonning Cutting. These 'Warships' were based on a successful German design.

scale orders. The first locomotive to be delivered under the pilot scheme was No. D8000 in June 1957. Built by English Electric, it had a 1,000 hp diesel engine with electric transmission and was intended for freight work. In the same year No. D5500 (diesels now had a special number series of their own), a 1,250 hp diesel-electric for passenger work, entered service. It was built by Brush of Loughborough. Both designs were excellent and eventually a total of well over 200 of each were bought by BR. Even today, nearly thirty years later, examples of both types remain at work.

Soon afterwards the British Transport Commission, urged on by the government, decided to speed up the modernization plan so as to reap its advantages more quickly. Steam was to be phased out completely within a few years. This meant far more diesels were needed than had originally been intended, and needed at once. The acceleration of dieselization was dramatic. In three years of the pilot scheme, from 1955 to 1958, 745 diesels had been built. Over the

next three years no less than 1,978 were taken into BR stock.

The readjustment from steam to diesel production took time, both within BR's own works and at those of the private companies. Steam had been perfected over many years, but the new diesels had to make it almost overnight. Inevitably there were disappointments along the way. Some of the most famous private builders, North British of Glasgow and Beyer Peacock in Manchester, for instance, found it all but impossible to divert their old steam skills into diesel production. Both firms went out of business in the 1960s.

The advantages of diesels over steam were much the same as for electrics. Both the new types of power were more economic to run as well as being cleaner and less polluting. The latter was important because the 1950s saw the introduction of 'smokeless zones' throughout the country. Industry and homes alike gradually turned away from coal with its associated killer fogs and smogs. A diesel was more economic because it could be ready for work at the turn of a switch. Steam's long unproductive hours during lighting up before or raking-out after each duty did not apply; a diesel could work almost 24 hours a day, seven days a week. In its 28 years of main line running *Mallard* notched up 1,426,261 miles. All 22 of the 'Deltic' diesels which took over on the East Coast route, however, had passed the two million miles mark after only 15 years! Diesels also needed more careful maintenance than steam, and new clean, light and spacious depots were built to house and repair them. The first all-diesel depot was at Devons Road, Bow, in East London. It presented a great contrast to the gloom and grime of most steam sheds.

As the swinging sixties dawned, modernization was at last beginning to make an impact. On 31st December 1960, there were 2,550 diesel locomotives, 135 electric locomotives, 6,442 electric train vehicles, and 3,833 diesel multiple-unit vehicles and railcars in service. Steam locomotives had been reduced to 13,271; less than

(*Above*) One of the Scottish Region's Blue Trains on trial at Craigendoran in 1960 before their introduction on the Glasgow Suburban system.

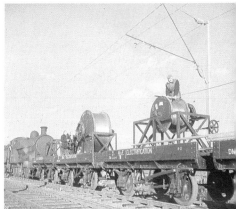

(*Above*) The old helps the new. An ancient LNWR 0–8–0 hauls a wiring train at Wilmslow on the first stretch of 25kV electrification between Crewe and Manchester.

(*Left*) 1160 hp Sulzer Type 2 diesel-electric No. D5030 prepares to leave its birthplace at Crewe in 1959.

(*Left*) Sparkling new: 3,300 hp class 'A' electric locomotive No. E3003, built in 1959 for the Crewe to Manchester/Liverpool lines.

(*Above*) Ancient and modern, a century separates Brunel's Royal Albert Bridge and the 'Warship' diesel-hydraulic crossing it with the 'Cornish Riviera Express'.

eight years later they would all have gone. Diesel locomotives were now grouped into five main types, though still based on power. These were Type 1 (800 to 1,000 hp); Type 2 (1,000 to 1,365 hp); Type 3 (1,500 to 1,750 hp); Type 4 (2,000 to 2,700 hp) and Type 5 (over 3,300 hp).

A diesel-electric locomotive is basically an electric loco carrying its own power plant around with it. It works by connecting the diesel engine to a generator which then drives the electric traction motors located on the bogies, and this turns the wheels. Instead of this electric transmission of power, it is also possible to use a hydraulic system. Here fluids, which cannot be compressed, are forced through defined channels to achieve the same effect. At the beginning of the modernization plan each region had a considerable freedom to build or order locomotives for its own services. The Western Region, carrying on a tradition for individuality that began with Brunel, chose diesel-hydraulic locomotives having been impressed by their performance on the German Federal Railway.

The original locomotives of the first two diesel-electric types to appear under the pilot scheme: (*Above*) is D8000 and (*Left*) is D5500. Both were built in 1957 and are now preserved.

(*Left*) *Deltic* was the prototype of the famous class of 22 3,300 hp diesel-electrics that bore its name. Built by English Electric in 1954, it is now in the Science Museum.

(*Above*) Inside the new diesel depot at Finsbury Park in 1960.

(*Left*) Two Metro-Vick Type 2 1,200 hp diesel-electrics roar out of London with the Glasgow-bound 'Condor' fast container train in 1959.

(*Above*) A four-car DMU, for St Pancras–Bedford local services.

(*Left*) No. D1 *Scafell Pike* was the first of the 2,300 hp 'Peak' class diesel-electrics introduced in 1959.

(*Right*)   No. D3093 was one of over 1,000 similar 350–400 hp 0–6–0 diesel-electric shunters built from 1953 onwards, to replace elderly steam engines.

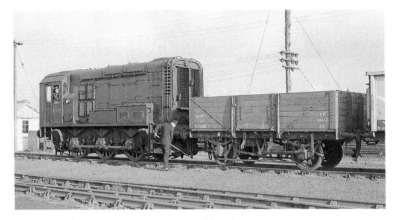

(*Above*)   Two of the luxury 'Blue Pullmans' built for the Western Region in 1960.

(*Below*)   In 1962 the Western Region switched from green to maroon for its main line diesels. This is 2,700 hp No. D1061 *Western Envoy* leaving Harbury tunnel the following year.

Needless to say everyone else went for diesel-electrics.

One-by-one the main routes began to switch to diesel power. On the Western Region the 'Warship' class diesel-hydraulics took over on the West Country trains starting in 1958. In the same year English Electric Type 4 diesel-electrics speeded up services on both the Liverpool Street–Norwich and King's Cross–Sheffield routes. Within two years they were in control of both East and West Coast main line trains. The traditional rivalry seemed to be ended – for a while. There were many other less powerful types for semi-fast, or cross-country services. Diesel multiple-units (DMUs), two or three coaches permanently coupled together with underfloor power equipment, were used on branch lines and suburban routes not scheduled for electrification; inter-city versions were built for longer, faster runs such as Edinburgh–Glasgow.

Meanwhile, selected electrification schemes were underway. On 6th March 1956 the BTC had taken an important decision. This

(*Left*)   One of Western Region's last steam expresses, No. 7005 *Sir Edward Elgar* leaves Moreton-in-Marsh in 1961.

(*Above*)   Steam's final hours in the birthplace of the railways. Two freight engines simmer at West Hartlepool depot on 8th September 1967. Next day it was all over.

(*Above*)   Class 'A2' 4–6–2 No. 60532 *Blue Peter* blasts out of Edinburgh with a train to Aberdeen on 28th August 1966. A week later main line steam finished in Scotland.

(*Right*)   A grimy No. 45285 waits on the centre roads at Carlisle during the final summer of steam over Shap in 1967. No. D1622 is beside it.

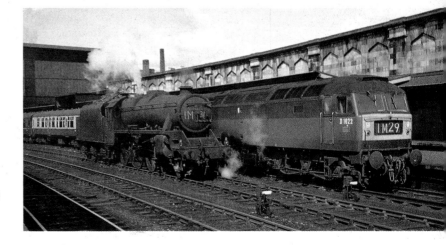

(*Left*) Steam's final main line workings were on the Weymouth route. Rebuilt Bulleid Pacific No. 34093, waits to leave Waterloo on 28th June 1967.

(*Above*) Standard class 5MT 4–6–0 No. 73117 leaves Southampton Ocean Terminal with a Waterloo boat train conveying passengers from the 'Queen Elizabeth'.

was to use the 25 kilovolt (kV) 50 cycle ac overhead system, which had proved successful in Europe, for all future main line electrification. The only exception was to be the Southern which would continue to expand its third-rail electrified network. The first sections of main line to be electrified on the 25 kV system were Crewe–Manchester on 12th September 1960 and Crewe–Liverpool on 1st January 1962. Very powerful 3,300 hp electric locomotives were built to work these trains. Painted in electric blue, with cut-out steel numbers and BTC lion-and-wheel emblem, they made an aggressively up-to-date sight. Suddenly modernization was beginning to work.

Electric multiple-units took over elsewhere. In 1959 the Southern Electric network was extended into Kent and a mere two years later steam had vanished from the county. On 16th March that year EMUs capable of 145 kph (90 mph) took over the lines from Liverpool Street to Colchester, Clacton and Walton-on-the-Naze. The following year Liverpool Street electrified its famous 'Jazz trains' to Enfield and Chingford, which had once been the busiest steam suburban service in the world. Many of Glasgow's suburban lines went electric on 7th November 1960 when the Blue Trains were introduced. These new wide-windowed EMUs provided standards of comfort not seen before on Scotland's local trains.

As modernization began to bite, steam locomotives went to the scrapyard in ever-increasing numbers. On 18th March 1960 there was a sad ceremony at Swindon Works. The 999th and last of the BR standards had come off the assembly line. It was also the last steam locomotive to be built by BR. In honour of this melancholy fact Western Region gave '9F' class 2-10-0 No. 92220 the ultimate Swindon accolade, a copper-capped chimney. And, although it was a freight locomotive, it was painted in lined-out passenger green

(*Above*) Until 1966 the Isle of Wight had a self-contained steam worked system. The engines were old LSWR class '02' 0–4–4Ts each named after an Island village.

(*Above*) No. 70013 *Oliver Cromwell* was the last of the 'Britannia's' in service, seen here in April 1968.

(*Left*) End of the line for steam. Sparks shower from class 4F 0–6–0 No. 43861 as it is cut up at Horwich Works.

and named. A competition was run in the WR's staff magazine to find a suitable name for this historic engine. The winning suggestion was *Evening Star*. It was most appropriate, for the second locomotive ever to run on the GWR had been named *Morning Star*. Now steam's long day was dying.

As the country shivered in the big freeze of winter 1962–63, BR began the most important decade in its history. On 1st January 1963 a new British Railways Board was created to replace the British Transport Commission, which was abolished. Chairman of the BRB was industrialist Dr Richard Beeching and his orders from the government were clear. They had been outlined in a speech by the Prime Minister, Harold Macmillan, to the House of Commons in

(*Above*) A station without rails. Fraserburgh in North East Scotland, in May 1969, four years after passenger trains had ceased.

(*Above*)   Two Brush Type 4 diesel-electrics (now class 47) in their original two-tone livery head a train of oil tank wagons. 512 of these engines were built from 1962 on.

(*Above*)   The wires go up over a steam landmark. An electrification construction train at Shap Summit is passed by a class 50 diesel-electric on a Freightliner train in 1973.

(*Right*)   Class 86/2 electric locomotives at Carlisle.

March 1960. 'The railway system must be remodelled to meet current needs and the modernization plan must be adapted to this new shape . . . This will involve certain sacrifices . . . for example in the reduction of uneconomic services.'

It was to be a new face for a new age. Britain itself had changed from the drab grey years following the Second World War. By the late 1950s most people were better off than they had ever been. It was a time of full employment and the older industries found it difficult to recruit staff. No one wanted a job cleaning dirty old steam locomotives.

For the first time washing machines, televisions and foreign holidays were within the reach of the average working person. Macmillan himself summed it up in a sentence that turned out to be the catch phrase for a generation: 'many people have never had it so good,' he remarked. Cars were now being mass-produced at a price most people could afford. In 1938 there had been 1.9 million cars on Britain's roads, by 1957 the figure was 4.2 million and just four years later it had risen to 6.3 million. A second transport

revolution was underway with cars, heavy lorries and internal airlines all gnawing away at BR's passenger and freight business.

On 27th March 1963, Beeching presented to Parliament a report called 'The Reshaping of British Railways'. The Beeching Report as it was immediately dubbed by the newspapers was a bombshell. Lines and stations which lost money were to be closed. The remainder of the rail network was to be pulled firmly together into a tight economic system that did what it was best at — transporting passengers and freight over long distances at high speeds, and carrying intensive commuter services. Since the Beeching plan over 10,000 km (6,000 miles) of track and 4,000 stations have been abandoned. It was railway mania in reverse. Interestingly, the railway map of the mid 1970s began to resemble that of the 1850s. The main lines which had been built first proved still to be the most important well over a century later. In its present form as part of the West Coast route, Robert Stephenson's London & Birmingham Railway is still one of BR's most profitable routes.

Many of the lines that were closed dated from the years of wasteful competition after the 1870s. In 1899 the Manchester, Sheffield & Lincolnshire Railway opened a brand new main line into London, the last to reach the capital, and changed its name to the Great Central Railway. Even then there were doubts about the financial wisdom of such a move. If, said the cynics at the time, MS&L stood for 'Money Sunk and Lost' then GC meant 'Gone Completely'! This last main line closed down on 3rd September 1966, leaving only a suburban service from Marylebone to Aylesbury.

Steam was now in its death throes. An ever-increasing band of enthusiasts chased round the country intent on seeing, photographing and worshipping steam before it disappeared forever.

On 3rd August 1968, the 21.25 Preston to Liverpool Exchange was crowded with passengers wearing black ties, as Stanier 'Black Five' 4-6-0 No. 45318 headed the very last scheduled steam-hauled passenger train. At the end of the following day steam finished in regular service. Exactly a week later, BR ran a commemorative special to mark the end of standard gauge steam. It started and finished at Liverpool Lime Street, passing through the great Olive Mount cutting where, during its construction 140 years previously, navvies had hung like flies on the bare walls. The special traversed the raw splendour of the Settle & Carlisle before finally returning over Stephenson's pioneer Liverpool & Manchester line. With 'Black Five' 4-6-0 No. 45110 in charge it paused briefly at Rainhill, where *Rocket* had once astonished the world, and then it was gone with only a trail of steam to mark its passing.

The end of steam was the opportunity to rethink the whole appearance of BR. In 1964 its name was shortened to British Rail and the famous double arrow symbol devised as part of a new corporate identity. A universal look was created for the entire system. Restyled signs with black lettering on a white background replaced the old regional colours. Rail blue became the standard colour for all locomotives. During 1956 the WR had repainted

(*Above*)   InterCity electrics pass at Watford Gap. How little space the railway takes compared to the adjacent M1.

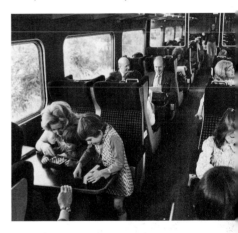

(*Above*)   Passenger comfort in the seventies. A second class air-conditioned Mark 11D carriage.

(*Above*)   During its final years the 'Golden Arrow' boat train was hauled by one of SR's few electric locomotives.

(*Above*) A diesel locomotive legend at speed. One of the 3,300 hp 'Deltics' which hauled the crack East Coast Main Line expresses for nearly 20 years.

(*Above*) A class 86/2 heads an InterCity train of mainly air-conditioned stock on the West Coast Main Line.

certain carriages in chocolate and cream; the SR had reverted to green and other coaches were given a maroon livery. Now all main line vehicles were to be rail blue and grey. Suburban stock would be just blue. A new era was beginning.

During the 1960s, speeds of 160 kph (100 mph) became an everyday event at last on certain sections of BR. The first loco-motives to achieve this distinction were the 'Deltics' — 22 ultra-powerful 3,300 hp diesel-electrics that quickly became a locomotive legend. Their triangular-shaped engines were designed originally for use in naval gun boats and for a while they were the world's most powerful single-unit diesels. The 'Deltics' entered service on the East Coast main line where they displaced 55 Pacifics in 1961. A year later they speeded up Anglo Scottish schedules. Long stretches of the East Coast route had their top speed raised to 160 kph (100 mph) and for the first time ordinary passengers were doing the ton on scheduled trains.

The second great acceleration took place on 18th April 1966 when electrification was completed between Euston and Crewe. Through electric services between London and Manchester and Liverpool cut timings from around 4 hours to 2¾ hours. On 6th March 1967 the wires were extended to Coventry, Birmingham and Wolver-hampton. Everywhere the new superfast, clean, comfortable trains were a great success and people swarmed to travel on them. A great new station at Euston grew from the ashes of the old haphazard Victorian buildings, and was opened by the Queen on 14th October 1968.

Eventually government permission was given to BR to push the wires on to their logical destination — Glasgow. Completed on 6th May 1974 the 'Electric Scots' were another great boost for the West Coast main line. The Euston to Glasgow journey was brought down to only five hours as the great steam-age obstacles of Shap and

Beattock banks were ironed out. Up front were the new 5,000 hp Class 87 electric locomotives, the most powerful on BR.

Other modernization was going ahead at full speed too. A new, more comfortable Mark II coach was introduced in 1964, and on 12th July 1971 an air-conditioned version was put into service on the King's Cross–Newcastle route. Four years later, on 12th May 1975, passengers settled down in Euston–Liverpool trains made up of the very latest Mark III design. These 24 m long (75 foot long) coaches feature not only air-conditioning but double glazing, wall-to-wall carpeting and sound insulation as well.

In the fifteen years from 1960 to 1975 freight trains were transformed. The old slow line of clanking wagons with no continuous brakes disappeared. In its place were fast, fully-braked, modern, high-capacity vehicles capable of running at 120 kph (75 mph). Private sidings were built in factories, so that bulk loads could be transferred straight into the train. Freightliners, introduced on 15th November 1965, combined rail's great speed and economy for long hauls with road's flexibility for local delivery. Box-shaped containers were transferred between road and rail vehicles at special terminals where Freightliner trains began or ended their journeys.

Safety was uppermost in everyone's mind as the modernization of signalling equipment continued. As long ago as 1902 the London & South Western Railway had used pneumatic power rather than manually operated levers to set signals. Electrically operated colour-light signals were introduced from the 1930s onwards, and their installation on main lines was speeded up under the modernisation plan. Today one large power signalbox can do the work of dozens of the old manual boxes. A signalman has only to turn a switch to set automatically the route for a train over many miles of

(*Above*)   The Bournemouth line was electrified in July 1967 using these 4–TC EMUs.

(*Below*)   The concourse of the new Euston station opened in 1968.

(*Above*) Both bound for Euston. A class 310 EMU on an outer suburban service is overtaken by a class 86/2 electric locomotive hauling an InterCity express in September 1973.

(*Below*) A DMU on the Paddington suburban service sports the white livery used on local trains for a short time during the late 1970s.

track. Above his control panel the train's passage is indicated by red lights on an illuminated route diagram. The line is still divided into sections but the colour-light signals change automatically to danger once a train has passed. Like its predecessors colour-light signalling is failsafe. If anything goes wrong with the system every signal turns to red.

Another important signalling safety measure is AWS, which stands for Automatic Warning System. Powerful magnets linked to the signals are laid between the rails. When a locomotive passes over them it makes contact, and if the signal is clear, a bell rings in the driver's cab. Should the signal be at danger a horn sounds and unless the driver cancels it the brakes come on automatically.

The basic idea of this audible cab signalling, as it is sometimes called, dates back to the GWR who introduced a similar system on 1st January 1906. All main lines are now being fitted with AWS and colour-light signalling.

As very high speeds became commonplace, improvements in main line track also took place. CWR (continuous welded rail) has replaced the old individual 19 m (60 feet) length rails. Now rails are welded together in lengths of up to 402 m (1,320 feet), and laid on long-lasting concrete sleepers rather than wooden ones. The combination of CWR and concrete sleepers gives a much smoother, quieter (no more clickety-clacking) ride for the passenger and is much easier to maintain.

Twenty years after it had first been announced, the benefits of the modernization plan were there for all to see. And in the wake of the great energy crisis of 1973 passengers were returning to the railways in ever-increasing numbers, their cars abandoned as petrol prices rocketed. The gouged-out motorways of the 1960s had despoiled much of Britain's countryside and people began to react against them. There was opposition too to the destruction caused by the continuous stream of heavy lorries that crashed their way through the narrow streets of historic towns and villages. Freight, people said, was for the rails not for the roads.

The modern electric and diesel railway was realized to be very fast, very quiet, very efficient, easy on the environment and very energy saving. 'Let the train take the strain' invited the posters, so people did. And, by the mid 1970s, there was a train waiting in the wings that would prove a world beater for British Rail.

(*Above*)   Contrast in signalling. The manually-operated signalbox at Warrington.

(*Above*)   Victoria signalling centre at Clapham Junction. This is the newest power signalbox on the Southern Region and was opened in 1984.

(*Left*)   London Bridge station with the power signalbox on the left of the picture.

11 Age of the supertrain

At exactly 18.45 on the warm summer's evening of 30th August 1984, Driver Harry Rail opened the controller on his High Speed Train and shot out of Paddington station. Three miles and three minutes later the sleek blue and yellow train was racing along at just under 160 kph (100 mph); 14 km (9 miles) out of London it was hitting 200 kph (125 mph). A mere 62 minutes and 33 seconds after leaving Paddington, Harry Rail was drawing to a halt under the great roof of Bristol Temple Meads station. The 189.2 km (117.6 miles) had been covered at an average speed of 181.3 kph (112.7 mph), the fastest ever start-to-stop journey by a diesel train between two major cities.

The record-breaking run was filmed by BBC Television and transmitted live during its Top of the Pops programme. Jimmy Savile travelled on the train and later named the leading HST powercar, No. 43002, *Top of the Pops*. A number one performance all round! That night 20 million viewers were given a glimpse of the raw power of BR's supertrains. Away from the limelight the High Speed Trains (HSTs for short) are no less fast. Each day up to 95 of these supertrains race across Britain, from Penzance to Inverness, covering much of the distance at 200 kph (125 mph).

Age and the supertrain. An InterCity 125 High Speed Train glides smoothly through the ancient buildings of Bath.

(*Left*) The prototype High Speed Train during trials on the Western Region. It holds the world speed record for a diesel.

(*Above*) The view from the cab as two High Speed Trains pass at speed.

The HST story began in the early 1970s, and by 1973 a prototype train was undergoing rigorous tests. On 6th June that year it touched 214 kph (133 mph) to smash *Mallard's* long-standing record and become the fastest train in Britain. Five days later, on 11th June, the silver grey prototype was raced up to an outstanding 226.9 kph (141 mph), held for over a mile between Thirsk and Tollerton on the East Coast main line. It was a world speed record for a diesel, and it's a record that the HSTs still hold.

On 4th October 1976 the new high speed era dawned for BR and its customers. Production series HSTs swept effortlessly into action on the Paddington to Bristol and South Wales routes on schedules that were out of this world. For the first time there was a regular

(*Above*) Inside one of an HST's Mark III carriages.

(*Left*) A production series InterCity 125 High Speed Train in the original yellow and blue livery.

service of trains running at 160 kph (100 mph) average start to stop. Passenger reaction was immediate and enthusiastic — the supertrains were a hit! Since then HSTs have introduced InterCity 125 standards on the Paddington to Plymouth and Penzance, King's Cross to Edinburgh, Aberdeen and Inverness, King's Cross to Leeds and Bradford, and St Pancras to Sheffield routes. They are also a familiar sight on the main trains over the great railway heartline from Scotland and the North East to the South West via Birmingham.

An HST has two power cars, each fitted with a 2,250 hp Paxman Valenta engine, and situated at either end of the train for quick turnarounds. Between the power cars are seven or eight Mark III coaches all with air-conditioning, double glazing, wall to wall carpets and automatic connecting doors. Every train has a restaurant or buffet car where you can buy high-speed snacks such as hamburger and chips. Fast food never came faster than on an HST! And, in the age of the supertrain, there is absolutely no time for hanging around. HSTs notch up the kilometres at an incredible rate compared to the old days. At least one HST unit travels over 1,600 km (1,000 miles) in a single day. Compare that to the maximum of around 850 km (540 miles) possible with steam in its heyday.

The British supertrains operate on ordinary tracks, shared with other services, unlike the high-speed trains of France and Japan which need expensive purpose-built routes just for them. And the InterCity 125 is the only high speed train in the world to have won an export order. A slightly modified version is now in service on the railways of New South Wales in Australia. HSTs aren't the only BR trains to top 160 kph (100 mph). On the West Coast route the 5,000 hp Class 87 electric locomotives have been fitted with new pantographs which allow them to run at 177 kph (110 mph).

(*Above*) Fast food – the buffet car on an InterCity 125.

(*Above*) Commuters arriving at Waterloo. The class 508 EMUs have now been transferred to the Merseyrail service.

(*Left*) The newest EMUs for Waterloo suburban services are these class 455 units. All new suburban trains now have sliding doors.

(*Right*) A class 317 EMU built for the Midland suburban electrification in 1983 runs over a section of concrete paved track near Kings Cross.

(*Above*) Birmingham International station opened in 1977 to serve the airport and National Exhibition Centre.

(*Above*) Racehorses have long been popular subjects for locomotive names but this was probably the first time one attended a naming ceremony.

As train speeds are increased, journey times are cut and more passengers are attracted to the advantages of rail travel. Long distances at high speeds: to many passengers it's what the railway of today is all about. But it's not the whole story. British Rail runs more than 15,000 passenger trains carrying nearly two million people between over 2,300 stations — every day. Many of these passengers are commuters. Each weekday morning almost 400,000 people pour into London in the space of just a couple of hours. And every evening they go back home again. Faster services on InterCity lines mean people can live further and further away and yet still be within reasonable travelling time of their place of work. Commuting from Peterborough for instance, 122 km (76 miles) away, is no problem now that it can be done in 50 minutes by HST.

New, modern, comfortable, sliding-door trains have been introduced on suburban lines in Glasgow, London and Merseyside. Major electrification schemes in the last ten years include in London the Great Northern suburban (King's Cross and Moorgate to Welwyn Garden City, Hertford and Royston) and the Midland suburban (St Pancras and Moorgate to Bedford). Each has a feature unique on BR. When the GN line was electrified through from Drayton Park to Moorgate its route was over a former Underground line. Unfortunately the tunnels were too small to take the overhead wires used everywhere else. The new Class 313 EMUs were fitted with third-rail pick-up equipment for this section, as well as pantographs to collect current out in the open. If you stand at Drayton Park station you will see trains enter using one method and leave using the other. The Midland's claim to fame is that it has BR's first driver-only trains. There are no guards and the automatic doors are operated by the driver who is in direct radio contract with the signalboxes along the route.

In many rural areas BR run trains which are a great lifeline to the local people, but do not carry enough passengers to cover their costs. BR has an agreement with the government who pay the cost of these services because they are of benefit to the whole community.

Railfreight is a £500 million business that carries everything from pet food to petrol, quickly, cleanly and without damage to the environment. Whatever the load, railways remain the best way of transporting large quantities of goods over long distances. Department of Energy studies show that rail is three times as energy efficient as road in moving bulk supplies. Just one freight train can carry a load that would need a convoy of roadcrunching lorries to do the job. Merry-Go-Round is a continuous operation bringing coal directly from pit to power station like a mobile conveyor belt. MGR trains can carry up to 1,000 tonnes of coal each and unload while still on the move, at 1 kph (½ mph). It's Railfreight at its best.

Faith in Railfreight is shown by many companies who have their own special wagons which run to and from sidings laid straight into their factories. New heavy freight locomotives, the 3,300 hp Class

(*Above*)   A class 507 EMU on the Merseyrail system.

(*Below*)   Two of the powerful class 56 diesel-electrics exert a combined horsepower of 6,500 and enter Llanwern Steelworks with a train of iron-ore from Port Talbot Docks in July 1979.

(*Left*) Railfreight's newest locomotives are the 3,300 hp class 58 diesel-electrics introduced in 1982.

58 and 3,250 hp Class 56 diesel-electrics, have been built to handle this important traffic. The Class 58s can hit 130 kph (80 mph) with a 1,000 tonne load. No wonder railway enthusiasts call them the 'thousand-tonne flyers'.

The location of any freight wagon is available at the touch of a button thanks to a system that's just TOPS. Total Operations Processing System links freight yards throughout the country to a central computer in London. Information on all freight movements and the rolling stock involved is fed in and can be extracted by any BR operator. TOPS has recently been extended to cover locomotives as well, and coaches will be included soon.

But whether it's carrying people or rubbish (no offence, every day Railfreight neatly disposes of the contents of a million dustbins), BR has to spread the message that rail is best. Television and posters advertise what BR has to offer. All kinds of special tickets and Railcards are tailor-made to make rail travel easier and cheaper for different types of people.

Tourists are people who want to see Britain at its finest and nowhere does it look better than from a train. Many railway lines go through magnificent scenery and often are the only way of seeing the best bits! BR are also opening completely new stations with financial help from local authorities, and reopening others. Towns and villages develop all the time and require good transport as their population increases. A station is the obvious answer.

Some of these new stations are Parkways. Situated on the edge of large towns or cities, they let motorists drive a short distance from home then pick up an InterCity train for the rest of their journey. Motorail, where passengers and their cars both travel by train, helps the holidaymaker avoid long gruelling drives, from London to Scotland, for instance. With 15.9 million cars crowded on to Britain's roads BR has to help ease the load somehow!

Certain traditionally railway-linked operations have recently been sold off at government request leaving BR to concentrate on running

(*Above*) Filling a Merry-Go-Round train with coal at a colliery. When it reaches the power station the coal will be discharged automatically.

trains. Sealink, the railway-owned shipping service, was sold in 1984. A cross-channel hovercraft service, started by BR in 1968, has also gone, as have all the railway hotels.

But one link with the past has grown stronger over the last decade. BR never completely did away with steam. Since 1968 it has continued to run the tiny narrow gauge Vale of Rheidol Railway. And, as standard gauge steam finished in regular service, people rushed to preserve it. Groups of enthusiasts all over Britain bought short lines to operate as living museums. Steam, like so many aspects of our industrial past, is now an entertainment.

On 27th September 1975, exactly 150 years after *Locomotion* set out on its historic first journey, the Duke of Edinburgh opened the National Railway Museum. Located in the former York North engine depot, the NRM is a joy to railway enthusiasts and casual visitors alike. Locomotives and carriages sit gleaming in the glory of a dozen pre-grouping liveries, and are supplemented by many other exhibits depicting the British railway heritage, past and present, ranging from waistcoat buttons to nameplates and posters.

Each day the InterCity 125 HSTs, the supertrains, roll in and out of the great vaulted arch that covers York station. They are the railway of today. As they pass the nearby museum they salute the sleeping giants of yesterday's railway. George Stephenson was once described as 'a maniac fit only for Bedlam' because he suggested trains might reach 32 kph (20 mph). Now British Rail runs more trains at 160 kph (100 mph) during their journey than any other railway in the world. This is the age of the supertrain!

(*Above*) Transferring a container from road to rail at a Freightliner depot.

(*Below*) The scenic railway. A DMU crosses Barmouth Bridge on the Cambrian coast line in mid-Wales.

12 Next station

The best news for British Rail in 25 years. That was everyone's reaction to the government's 1984 green light for BR to go electric on the East Coast main line. Around £306 million is being spent electrifying the 627 km (390 miles) from Hitchin to Edinburgh, including the Doncaster–Leeds line, and re-equipping the entire InterCity service with new locomotives and rolling stock. A full 15 minutes will be clipped off present journey times of 4½ hours between the two capitals. But speed is not the main advantage of this electrification scheme. An all-electric ECML will save £80 million a year on maintenance. Reliability of rolling stock will be 50 to 70 per cent better and, as electricity is cheaper than diesel, fuel costs will be cut by a quarter too. Target dates for completion of this great enterprise are November 1989 to Leeds, and May 1991 for full electric services to Edinburgh.

The fastest train ever to run in Britain is the InterCity Development Train, better known as the APT (Advanced Passenger Train).
(*Inset*) A model of the proposed class 91 'Electra' locomotive for InterCity 225 services of the future.

(*Above*)   British Rail's most powerful locomotives are the 5,000 hp class 87s, introduced in 1974.

(*Above*)   Class 86/2 No. 86242 *James Kennedy G.C.* has the final InterCity colours with a wide black band below the cab windows.

Electrification — quieter, smoother, cheaper and more efficient — is the future InterCity routes. Other schemes in progress will bring the live wires to Norwich and Cambridge. Another will extend the Southern's third-rail network to the Tonbridge–Hastings line. All are due for completion by 1987.

New trains will be needed for the new electric railways. Much of the vital basic research has been done using BR's InterCity development train, better known perhaps as the Advanced Passenger Train or APT, the famous tilting train. The APT-P prototype became the fastest train ever to run in Britain when, on 20th December 1979, it reached 257.4 kph (160 mph) during trials. This was on the Euston to Glasgow line, where five years later, on 12th December 1984, it reeled off the whole 645.8 km (401.4 miles) in 232 minutes at an average speed of 165.7 kph (103 mph). The real breakthrough made by the APT, however, is its ability to tilt as it goes round curves. This means they can be taken at higher speeds without discomfort or danger to passengers. Extra speed round curves is just as important for reducing journey times as ultra high speeds on straight sections of track. It's the best way of fitting tomorrow's supertrains on to a railway laid out for the low speeds of 150 years ago.

A tremendous amount of valuable information has been obtained from the APT experiment. It will be put into practice in a few years' time when InterCity 225 services start on the West Coast route. Tilting coaches, based on the APT, will be hauled by Class

91 'Electra', 225 kph (140 mph) locomotives. An experimental 6,000 hp Class 89 electric locomotive is also planned for comparison tests.

In the meantime existing Mark III coaches are getting a facelift with bright new interiors. A new InterCity livery of two shades of grey with red and black stripes is being applied to the outsides of both locomotives and coaches.

The name InterCity first appeared in 1951 on a solitary London to Wolverhampton express. In 1966 it became the brand name for all BR's prestige main line trains. Now it is also the most important of BR's 'Sectors'. There are five sectors, covering InterCity, Railfreight, Parcels, London & South East and Provincial Services. Each is run as a separate countrywide business regardless of regional boundaries.

Bright new trains are racing down the tracks on provincial services too. Called Sprinters, these blue and grey diesel units are high-speed runners with a 120 kph (75 mph) maximum. Nearly 200 two-car trains are planned for cross-country services where they will replace the ageing fleet of DMUs, all of which are now over 20 years old. New lightweight railbuses are also under construction for use on local lines.

A second great industrial revolution has been brought about by the invention of the microchip. BR has seized with enthusiasm the unlimited opportunities offered by high technology and is using it to plan the railway of the twenty-first century. A microprocessor-based signalling system is under trial for eventual use on InterCity routes. Radio signalling using coded signals from a central control box direct to a visual display unit in the locomotive's cab has been developed for lines with relatively few trains. Visual display equipment to show the train's maximum permitted speed at any point during a journey has been tried out on the Advanced Passenger

(*Above*)   The video lounge on the overnight 'Starlight Express' which runs between Euston and Glasgow.

(*Above*)   New colour schemes inside for InterCity carriages too.

(*Left*)   An InterCity 125 High Speed Train in its new colours.

(*Above*) Class 50 diesel-electric No. 50023 *Howe* at Waterloo with an Exeter train. This style of livery was introduced on some engines before the new InterCity colours became standard.

Train. Computers are used for route setting in power signalboxes, for booking and reservations systems, in the design of new rolling stock and of course in TOPS. PETS is tops too. It stands for Passenger Enquiry Terminals and allows travellers to obtain train information at the touch of a button.

Higher speeds, increased comfort, even greater safety, improved efficiency, lower costs, better value to the community — all these are being achieved now by the railway of today. For the railway of tomorrow new targets must be set. If George Stephenson could return to life it seems likely that the father of the railways would recognize his grown up brainchild. He would certainly be astounded by its progress. Steel wheels race over steel rails at far higher speeds than he ever imagined, but the principle is the same.

Other methods have been suggested often, and there is always talk about a hovertrain. It would float on air between two opposing magnets guided along a great central monorail. So far the idea has progressed no further in Britain than a low-speed people mover for Birmingham Airport. But this uses a suspension system designed by BR's Research & Development team in a bold engineering leap that rivals Trevithick's. Perhaps maglev, as it's called, is today's *Catch me who can*, gliding quietly along and dreaming of greater things.

One day when the oil finally runs out and Britain's choked roads grind to a standstill, the railway will still be there.

Trains of today . . . and tomorrow?

(*Above*) A class 141 Railbus used on local services in Yorkshire.

(*Left*) A real smooth runner – a class 150 'Sprinter' introduced in 1984. 200 'Sprinters' are being built to replace DMUs on routes throughout the country.

(*Right*) The shape of things to come – perhaps. The magnetic levitation vehicle test track built by British Rail at its Derby Research Centre.

British Rail fact file

In 1983 695,200,000 train journeys totalling an estimated 30,095,000,000 km (18,700,000,000 miles) were made by passengers on British Rail. The average fare for each journey was £1.63 and the total money received in fares by British Rail that year was £1,137,500,000. At the end of the year British Rail had the following totals:

Locomotives and rolling stock

Diesel Locomotives	2,603
Electric Locomotives	247
HST Power Cars	197
APT Power Cars	6
Passenger Coaches (Locomotive Hauled)	4,059
(This includes 351 catering vehicles and 212 sleeping cars)	
Diesel Multiple Units	2,703
Electric Multiple Units	7,306
HST Coaches	709
APT Coaches	30
Freight Wagons	54,510

Route open for traffic

	km	miles
Passengers and freight	13,190	8,196
Passengers only	1,184	736
Freight only	2,589	1,609
Total route open for traffic	16,963	10,541

3750 km (2330 miles) of route electrified

Track open for traffic

	km	miles
Running lines	33,778	20,989
Sidings	7,524	4,675
Total track open for traffic	41,302	25,664

9920 km (6164 miles) of track electrified

Stations open for passengers ... 2,363
Plus 253 open for freight traffic only.

Highest Station	Corrour, Highland Region, 410.5 m (1347 ft)
Station with most platforms	London, Waterloo — 21
Longest station platform	Gloucester — 602.6 m (1,977 ft)

Busiest junction	Clapham Junction — about 2,000 trains every weekday
Longest tunnel	Severn Tunnel — 7,070 m (4 miles 628 yds)
Longest bridge	Tay Bridge — 3,460 m (2 miles 264 yds)
Bridge with longest span	Forth Bridge — 2 spans each 521.2 m (1710 ft)
Highest railway bridge	Ballochmyle Viaduct, Strathclyde Region, 49.9 m (164 ft) above river bed
Highest altitude reached by a section of line	Druimuachdar — 452.3 m (1484 ft) above sea level
Lowest point reached by a section of line	Severn Tunnel — 43.9 m (144 ft) below sea level
Steepest main line gradient	Lickey Incline (Birmingham — Bristol line) 1 in 37.7
Steepest gradient on any line	Merseyrail line into St James Street Station, Liverpool, 1 in 27

Travellers-Fare fact file (1983)

Number of daily trains with catering facilities	over 800
Number of meals sold on trains	1,083,400
Number of cups of coffee sold, on trains	8,201,000
on stations	10,500,000
Number of cups of tea sold, on trains	5,142,000
on stations	24,000,000
Number of sandwiches sold, on trains	3,141,000
on stations	8,638,000
Number of Casey Jones hamburgers sold	5,000,000

Index